BIG
IDEAS
OF SCIENCE
REFERENCE LIBRARY

PEARSON

BIG
IDEAS
OF SCIENCE
REFERENCE LIBRARY

PEARSON

Boston, Massachusetts
Chandler, Arizona
Glenview, Illinois
Upper Saddle River, New Jersey

ISBN-13: 978-0-13-369867-1
ISBN-10: 0-13-369867-X

11 V057 14 13

CONTENTS

KEY
These symbols appear in the top right corner below the topic name to connect the topic to the branches of science.

 Earth Science　　 Life Science　　 Physical Science

BIG IDEAS OF EARTH SCIENCE 🌎

The Big Ideas of earth science help us understand our changing planet, its long history, and its place in the universe. Earth scientists study Earth and the forces that change its surface and interior.

Earth is part of a system of objects that orbit the sun.

Asteroids
Astronomy Myths
Bay of Fundy
Comets
Constellations
Earth
Gravity
Jupiter's Moons
Mars
Mars Rover
Mercury
Meteorites
Moon
Neptune
Pluto
Saturn
Solar Eclipse
Solar Power
Space Probes
Summer Solstice
Uranus
Venus

Earth is 4.6 billion years old and the rock record contains its history.

Atmosphere
Dating Rocks
Deep Sea Vents
Dinosaurs
Eryops
Extinction
Family Tree
Fossils
Geologic Time
Giant Mammals
Ice Age

Earth's land, water, air, and life form a system.

Altitude
Atacama Desert
Atmosphere
Aurora Borealis
Buoys
Doppler Radar
Dust Storms
Earth's Core
Floods
Fog
Gliding
Predicting Hurricanes
Rainbows
Sailing
Snowmaking
Storm Chasing
Thunderstorms
Weather Fronts

Earth is the water planet.

Amazon River
Beaches
Drinking Water
Everglades
Great Lakes
Mid-Ocean Ridge
Niagara Falls
Ocean Currents
Sea Stacks
Surfing
Thermal Imaging
Tsunami
Upwelling
Water

Earth is a continually changing planet.

Acid Rain
Afar Triangle
Caves
Coal

Colorado Plateau
Colorado River
Coral Reefs
Crystals
Dunes
Earthquakes
Equator
Fluorescent Minerals
Geocaching
Geodes
Geysers
Glaciers
Gold Mining
Hoodoos
Ice Age
Islands
Kilauea
Landslides
Lava
Mapping
Marble Quarries
Mid-Ocean Ridge
Mount Everest
Niagara Falls
Rain Forest
Rubies
Sea Stacks
Soil
Terrace Farming
Tour de France
Tsunami

Human activities can change Earth's land, water, air, and life.

Air Pollution
Energy Conservation
Equator
Fuel Cell Cars
Global Warming
Ice Age
Ocean Currents
Rain Forest
Shelter

The universe is very old, very large, and constantly changing.

Big Bang Theory
Black Holes
Constellations
Hubble Space Telescope
Milky Way
Quasars
Universe

Science, technology, and society affect each other.

Astronauts
Hubble Space Telescope
Jetpacks
International Space Station
Mars Rover
Predicting Hurricanes
Robots
Satellite Dish
Science at Work
Space Technology
Space Tourism
Virtual World

Scientists use mathematics in many ways.

Buoys
Doppler Radar
Mars Rover
Measurement
Neptune

Scientists use scientific inquiry to explain the natural world.

Extinction
Predicting Hurricanes
Wind Power
Neptune

BIG IDEAS OF LIFE SCIENCE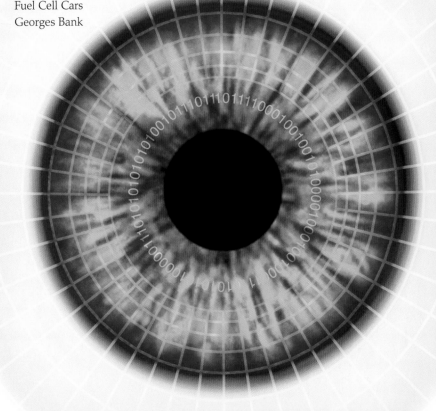

Life scientists study organisms, their life processes, and how they interact with one another and their environment. The Big Ideas of life science help us understand how living things are organized, how they get and use energy, and how they reproduce.

Living things grow, change, and reproduce during their lifetimes.

Animal Communication
Bush Baby
Courtship Rituals
Echolocation
Gorillas
Hummingbirds
Hypothalamus
Instinct
Marsupials
Menstrual Cycle
Penguins
Pregnancy
Puberty
Sea Horse
Seals
Sleep
Sloth
Tasmanian Devil
Twins
Worms

Living things are made of cells.

Blood Types
Cactus
Cell Division
Microscopes
Quarks and Leptons
Scent Pollution
Skeletons

Living things are alike yet different.

Adaptations
Aerogels
Bacteria
Bats
Bears
Cactus
Common Cold
DNA Connections
Exoskeleton
Family Tree
Farming
Ferns
Flowers
Frankenfoods
Fungi
Geckos
Giant Mammals
Gila Monster
Insects
Jellyfish
Naming
Patterns in Nature
Plant Tricks
Rain Forest
Red Tide
Redwoods
Scent Pollution
Skeletons
Snakes
Soil
Spiders
Survival
Symmetry
Taco Science
Whales

Living things interact with their environment.

Acid Rain
Air Pollution
Amazon River
Atacama Desert
Bats
Bay of Fundy
Beaches
Biodiversity
Biofuels
Bush Baby
Butterflies
Camouflage
Coal
Colorado Plateau
Deep Sea Vents
Energy Conservation
Everglades
Farming
Forestry
Frozen Zoo
Fuel Cell Cars
Georges Bank

Global Warming
GPS Tracking
Great Lakes
Hybrid Vehicles
Insects
Islands
Kilauea
Light Bulbs
Mid-Ocean Ridge
Mount Everest
Oil Spills
Patterns in Nature
Plant Invasion
Plastic
Population Growth
Rain Forest
Recycling
Red Tide
Renewal
Sea Horse
Seaweed
Seed Bank
Sharks
Shelter
Skywalk

Sloth
Soil
Solar Power
Supercooling Frogs
Sushi
Upwelling
Vultures

Genetic information passes from parents to offspring.

Blood Types
Colorblindness
DNA Evidence
Frankenfoods
Frozen Zoo
Genetic Disorders
Human Genome Project
Hummingbirds
Mutations
Probability

Living things get and use energy.

Algae
Barracuda
Birds
Cell Division
Elephants
Hummingbirds
New Body Parts
Octopus
Scorpion
Sea Horse
Seals
Sour Milk
Tasmanian Devil
Teeth

Structures in living things are related to their functions.

ACL Tear
Aerobic Exercise
ALS
Altitude
Animal Bodies
Birds
Blood Pressure
Blood Types
Brain Power
Broken Bones
Defibrillators
Digestion
Dolphins
Drinking Water
Exoskeleton
Fats

Gliding
Hearing Loss
Heartbeat
Hummingbirds
Jellyfish
Kidney Transplant
Laser Eye Surgery
Left vs. Right Brain
Marsupials
No Smoking
Open-Heart Surgery
Prosthetic Limb
Scent Pollution
Sea Turtles
Simulators
Singing
Skeletons
Skin
Sleep
Sloth
Steroids
Superfoods
Teeth
The Bends
Tour de France
Tweeters and Woofers
Vitamins and Minerals
Weightlifting

Living things change over time.

DNA Connections
Family Tree
Gorillas
Islands
Madagascar
Racehorses

Living things maintain constant conditions inside their bodies.

Allergies
Astronauts
Cancer Treatment
Common Cold
HIV/AIDS
Malaria
Marathon Training
Mold
MRI
Pandemic
Rats
Rheumatoid Arthritis
Scent Pollution
Sleep
Thermal Imaging
Vaccines
Working Body

Scientists use mathematics in many ways.

Census
Estimation
Hazardous Materials
Measurement
Probability
Simulators

Science, technology, and society affect each other.

Biomimetics
Clinical Trials
DNA Evidence
Eye Scan
Human Genome Project
Prosthetic Limb
Robots
Science at Work
Truth in Advertising

Scientists use scientific inquiry to explain the natural world.

BPA
Crittercam
Forensics
Human Genome Project
Naming
Quarks and Leptons
Truth in Advertising

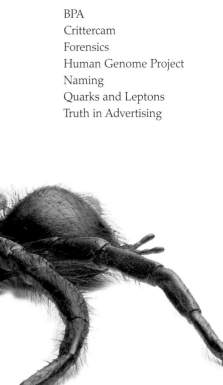

BIG IDEAS OF PHYSICAL SCIENCE

Physical scientists study matter and energy. The Big Ideas of physical science help us describe the objects we see around us and understand their properties, motions, and interactions.

A net force causes an object's motion to change.

Asteroids
Astronauts
Bridges
Collision
Crew
Drag Racing
Formula 1 Car
Gravitron
Gravity
Hockey
Hovercraft
Jetpacks
Meteorites
Quasars
Roller Coaster
Sailing
Skydiving
Snowboard
Tour de France

Energy can take different forms but is always conserved.

Aerogels
ALS
Aurora Borealis
Bicycles
Black Holes
Bridges
Bungee Jumping
Catapults
Cordless Drill
Crew
Defibrillators
Earth's Core
Energy Conservation
Geocaching
Gliding
Headphones
Hoover Dam
Hybrid Vehicles
Lichtenberg Figures
Lifting Electromagnets
Light Bulbs
Microscopes
MP3 Player
MRI
Niagara Falls
Radio
Roller Coaster
Rube Goldberg Devices
Skyscraper
Skywalk
Submarines
Taco Science
Thermal Imaging
Weightlifting

Waves transmit energy.

Animal Communication
Cellphone
Color
Digital Camera
Doppler Radar
Echolocation
Eye Scan
Fluorescent Minerals
Geocaching
GPS Tracking
Guitar
Headphones
Hearing Loss
Holograms
Hubble Space Telescope
Hummingbirds
Laser Eye Surgery
Lighthouse
Microscopes
Mirages
Night Vision Goggles
Predicting Hurricanes
Radio
Rainbows
Rubies
Satellite Dish
Sea Stacks
Seaweed
Singing
Solar Power
Sonic Booms
Surfing
Thunderstorms
Tsunami
Tweeters and Woofers
Virtual World

Atoms are the building blocks of matter.

Acid Rain
Black Holes
Body Protection
Caves
Creating Elements
Crystals
Geckos
Glass

Gold Mining
Mars Rover
Melting Point
Meteorites
Nuclear Medicine
Prosthetic Limb
Quarks and Leptons
Steel
The Bends
Water

Mass and energy are conserved during physical and chemical changes.

Digestion
Earth
Fire Extinguishers
Fireworks
Forestry
Hovercraft
Ice Houses
Lava
Melting Point
Scent Pollution
Snowmaking
Supercooling Frogs
The Bends

Scientists use mathematics in many ways.

Buoys
Hazardous Materials
Mars Rover
Measurement
Wind Tunnel

Scientists use scientific inquiry to explain the natural world.

Biomimetics
Forensics
Quarks and Leptons
Wind Power

Science, technology, and society affect each other.

Bridges
Cellphone
Formula 1 Car
Hubble Space
    Telescope
Light Bulbs
Prosthetic Limb
Robots
Science at Work

ACID RAIN

It can cause the paint to rub off your car. It can eat away stone buildings and sculptures, poison trees, and even kill entire lakes full of fish. You might think that only very concentrated acids can cause this kind of harm. However, given enough time, acid rain can be quite a threat. When power plants, cars, and factories burn fuel, they emit gases such as sulfur dioxide and nitrogen oxide. Volcanoes, forest fires, and decaying plants emit these gases, too. When these gases enter the atmosphere, they react with harmless gases to form sulfuric and nitric acids. These acids combine with water vapor and fall back to Earth in the form of acid rain. Acid-rain-forming gases can travel with winds for hundreds of miles. That means that acid rain can have expensive and deadly effects both locally and far from where it formed.

Built around 420 B.C., this porch decorates an ancient Greek temple at the Acropolis of Athens, Greece.

WEARING AWAY STONE ▶

Rain and other kinds of weather slowly break down rocks over time. Acid rain can speed up this process. Normal rain can have an acidity, or pH, of 6. Acid rain, on the other hand, can be ten times more acidic—with a pH of 5. Acids react with stones such as marble, limestone, and granite to form softer materials that crumble away over time.

did you
know?.....................
THE UNITED STATES PRODUCES MORE SULFURIC ACID THAN ANY OTHER CHEMICAL—ABOUT 40 MILLION TONS.

ACID BURNS ▼

Concentrated sulfuric acid is an oily, colorless liquid. When the acid comes in contact with this paper, it reacts with carbohydrates, such as cellulose—a fiber that comes from wood and other plants. In much the same way that a hot fire burns wood, the reaction removes water molecules and leaves behind black, soot-like carbon.

DESTROYING LIFE ▼

Acid rain that soaks into soil can dissolve and wash away nutrients that are important for plant growth. Trees weakened by acidic soil can lose their leaves. They can also become more susceptible to other environmental threats. Acid rain collects as runoff in rivers and lakes, killing fish and other aquatic organisms.

Just as concentrated acid burns this paper, weaker acid rain slowly poisons and disintegrates living and nonliving things.

Column sculpted
from solid marble

Until it was moved to
a museum, acid rain
was dissolving this
ancient work of art.

ACL TEAR

It's the last few seconds of your basketball team's championship game. You jump up to make a shot, but when you land on your feet, you hear a strange popping noise. Later your knee starts to swell up and turn black and blue. What happened? You may have torn your ACL—the anterior cruciate ligament in your knee. Ligaments are tough, fibrous bands of tissue that connect bones. The ACL is one of four ligaments inside the knee joint that connect the thighbone (femur) to the shinbone (tibia). The ACL keeps your bones in place, preventing the tibia from moving in front of the femur. It also keeps the joint from rotating too much. You can tear your ACL if you suddenly stop or change direction, twist your knee, or get hit from the side. No matter what causes the tear, however, you're not going to be playing sports for several months!

TWIST AND SHOUT ►

Every year, about 200,000 people in the United States injure their ACL. Most injuries happen when people are playing sports—particularly basketball, soccer, gymnastics, skiing, volleyball, and football—with lots of running, changing direction, or jumping. Getting tackled during football can also tear the ACL—but most tears happen without direct contact. Instead, the knee simply twists or straightens out too much.

did you know?...

ACL INJURIES DECREASED BY 88% WHEN A GROUP OF FEMALE SOCCER PLAYERS DID WARM-UP EXERCISES DESIGNED FOR PREVENTION.

SURGERY? ▶

After surgery for a torn ACL, most people have months of physical therapy. Surgery usually involves replacing the ACL with tissue from another part of the leg. This operation can create problems for growing children and teens because surgery involves reattaching the end of one bone to the end of another. To keep from damaging the growth plate on the end of the bone, doctors are developing new surgical techniques.

COMING UNHINGED

The knee works like a hinge. You can tear your ACL if you move this hinge beyond its normal range of motion.

The ACL and the PCL (posterior cruciate ligament) cross each other to connect the thighbone and the shinbone.

CRASH LANDINGS

ACL tears can happen if you twist your knee sideways while your foot is firmly planted facing forward or you straighten your leg out too much during a jump. It can also happen if you land awkwardly from a jump—for example, after making a layup in basketball or dismounting in gymnastics.

GENDER DIFFERENCES

Female athletes have up to eight times as many ACL injuries as male athletes. One reason is that their hips are wider, so the thigh bone connects to the knee at a sharper angle. This puts more pressure on the joint.

ADAPTATIONS

Fish that puff up like balloons, spiders that pose as ants, plants that eat meat: sometimes the adaptations that allow an organism to survive can be quite bizarre. But adaptations help plants and animals obtain food and water, keep safe, establish territory, withstand weather, and reproduce. We do not usually think of plants as meat-eaters, but some feed on insects, invertebrates, and even small mammals. These plants live in poor soils with few nutrients. They have special adaptations to attract, trap, kill, and digest their prey. These include sticky surfaces, and hinged leaves that snap shut when trigger hairs are touched. Anglerfish live in the deep ocean where it is totally dark. The females have a special spine on their dorsal fin, which hangs over their mouth and acts as a "fishing rod." The fleshy tip of this lure is often luminous to attract other fishes. Munch!

There is enough toxin in one of these fish to kill 30 adults—and there is no known antidote!

PUFFED AND POISONOUS ▶
Puffer fish and porcupine fish are slow swimmers, so they've had to develop other ways to stay safe from fast swimming predators. How? These impressive fish inflate themselves when they're threatened. They have incredibly elastic skin and can balloon up to about three times their normal size. Try swallowing this fish now, predator!

Porcupine fish are also armed with sharp spines from head to tail, making them even more difficult to attack.

Distinctive white spots help identify and camouflage the highly poisonous death puffer on the reef.

Special muscles rapidly pump water into the stomach to inflate the fish. The stomach can swell to 100 times its normal size.

Adaptations develop over generations, not during an individual's life.

The Venus' flytrap stays closed for about 10 days while it digests an insect.

Huge 18-inch (46-cm) tongues and extra thick saliva allow giraffes to eat their favorite leaves from thorny acacia trees.

Giraffes have special one-way valves in their long necks to regulate blood flow and stop them from fainting.

REACHING FOR THE SKY

Giraffes are the tallest animals of all, with long legs and necks that allow them to reach leaves up to 20 feet (6 m) high. To keep them from tipping over, giraffes have an unusual gait. They move the two legs on one side of the body forward, and then follow with the two legs on the other side. The giraffe's unusual shape also makes it awkward for them to lower their heads to drink, so they are more vulnerable to predators while they're drinking. Therefore, giraffes drink only about once a day, up to 10 gallons (40 L) each time.

did you know? SOME DESERT GECKOS HAVE FRINGED TOES THAT KEEP THEM FROM SINKING INTO SAND.

AEROBIC EXERCISE

On your mark, get set, go! You're off! You gulp air. Your heart pounds. Hey, wait—you have to run four laps of the football field. You pace yourself, and soon your breathing becomes more rhythmic. You are now in the aerobic zone, that is, "with oxygen." Your muscles can now convert nutrients to energy much more efficiently than they could without oxygen. Cells make energy without oxygen during short bursts of intense strengthening activity—such as sprinting or weight lifting. That process leaves waste products that make your muscles feel tired. During aerobic activity, your lungs take in extra oxygen and your heart pumps harder and faster to send that oxygen to your muscles. The main waste product is carbon dioxide, which you breathe out. Swimming, biking, jogging, and walking fast are just a few of the activities that get you into the aerobic zone.

Exercise releases endorphins in your brain. Endorphins are natural painkillers that help you feel happier and more relaxed.

DO IT YOUR WAY ▲

Exercise is aerobic when it makes you breathe hard and increases your heart rate for a sustained period of time, usually a minimum of 20 minutes. Activities can be aerobic at moderate intensity—brisk walking—or at vigorous intensity—jogging, rowing, or swimming. Your heart rate, or pulse, rises to a rate that is 60–85% of your maximum heart rate. Your maximum heart rate is roughly 220 beats per minute minus your age.

STRONGER, SMARTER, AND HAPPIER ▲

You probably know that exercise makes you stronger and keeps your weight down, but studies show that it also makes people smarter and happier. Regular exercise helps new cells grow in the hippocampus, the part of the brain that controls learning and memory. Health experts recommend 60 minutes of physical activity each day for children and teens.

did you know? DURING AEROBIC EXERCISE, YOU SHOULD BE ABLE TO TALK BUT NOT SING.

KEEP GOING ▶

If you just kept breathing, could you run or swim forever? Some marathon runners report "hitting the wall" at about 20 miles (about 32 km). Basically, they run out of stored energy and water, not oxygen. Still, athletes keep setting records. Slovenian Martin Strel set a record for the longest non-stop swim in 2001. He swam more than 313 miles (504 km) of the Danube River in just over 84 hours.

AEROGELS

This block of material is nicknamed "frozen smoke," but it is no gas. It's aerogel—a solid form of silica, the same compound that makes up glass and sand. One of aerogel's amazing properties is that it traps heat, so well that a block of aerogel can protect a human hand from the flame of a blowtorch. Aerogels are composed mostly of air. They start out as wet gels that are much like the gelatin that you eat for dessert. The wet gel is then dried under high temperatures and pressures. These conditions vaporize the liquid, leaving what is called a *matrix*. This is a jungle-gym-like network of silica molecules surrounding microscopic pockets of air. Aerogels are more than 90% air, making them excellent thermal insulators. A thermal insulator is a material that is a poor conductor of thermal energy. The trapped air inside the aerogel slows the transfer of heat so the heat stays in the aerogel instead of passing through it.

◄ WHITE OR CLEAR?

The smoky, white-blue appearance of aerogels does not come from color within the materials that make them up. Instead, the color comes from the scattering of light by the pockets of air trapped inside the matrix. Polar bear fur looks white for the same reason. There are no white pigments, or color molecules, in the fur. Each hair is a transparent, hollow tube filled with air. This trapped air is an effective thermal insulator, keeping these animals warm in their frigid environment.

▼ EFFECTIVE INSULATOR

If you want to keep your ice cream chilly and your house toasty warm, you have to slow the transfer of heat, or thermal energy, with a thermal insulator. Many types of thermal insulators—such as the foam panels that line a freezer and the fiberglass mats that fill the walls of many homes—rely on trapped air to slow the transfer of heat. Aerogels are used to insulate some extreme-weather jackets, blankets, sheets, windows, and skylights.

did you know? ASTRONOMERS USE AEROGEL AS "SPONGES" TO CAPTURE THE DUST FROM PASSING COMETS.

The flame of the blowtorch is hot enough to heat and melt the surface of the aerogel, but heat does not conduct far enough into the block to reach the hand.

The flame of a blowtorch can be higher than 2,300°F (1,300°C).

Because aerogels are made mostly of air, they also make great sponges. Researchers are looking into ways of using aerogels as water filters and even as sponges to soak up oil spills.

Aerogels hold the world record for the least dense solid—just slightly denser than air—yet they can support objects many times their own mass.

AFAR TRIANGLE

Blistering desert heat, miles of cracked earth spewing sulfur and lava, constant earthquakes, and almost no water—you have come to the Afar Triangle. This wedge of land, about the size of Nebraska, lies where Ethiopia borders the mouth of the Red Sea. Underneath the triangle, three giant pieces of Earth's crust meet in what is called a *triple junction.* The pieces, called *tectonic plates,* are pulling away from each other, stretching and thinning Earth's crust. Along the edges of the plates, volcanoes erupt. As the three plates drift apart, the land between the plates sinks. Some areas of the Afar Triangle are already more than 300 feet (100 m) below sea level. That is about as tall as a 30-story building! That's why many geologists call this area the Afar Depression.

SPLITTING UP ▼

The Afar Triangle is part of the East African Rift System, one of the largest systems of faults, or splits, in Earth's crust. Rifts are valleys that form when plates move apart. Over millions of years, one rift separated Africa and the Arabian Peninsula. Then the Red Sea filled in the gap. The rift forming in the Afar Triangle extends south beneath several East African countries. It could one day separate those countries from the rest of the continent.

Pools of sticky mud are all that remain after it rains in the Afar region, where one river barely supports the people who live along it.

When plates move apart, large cracks called *rifts* form.

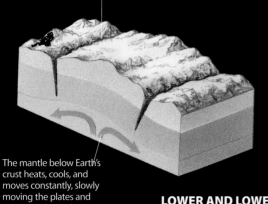

The mantle below Earth's crust heats, cools, and moves constantly, slowly moving the plates and changing the surface.

Mountains and highlands protect the Afar Triangle from flooding.

Lakes can form in open crevices and may even cool rising magma flows.

Small rifts form and then widen as the land continues to sink.

Volcanoes grow from magma that flows through jagged cracks and splits to the surface.

LOWER AND LOWER ▲

For now, low mountains to the east keep the Red Sea from flooding into the Afar Triangle, but these mountains are wearing down over time. Scientists predict that seawater will one day cover the Afar region.

did you know?......................
SOME OF THE OLDEST HUMAN-LIKE FOSSILS—MORE THAN 3 MILLION YEARS OLD—WERE FOUND IN THE AFAR REGION.

AIR POLLUTION

Cough, hack, wheeze! Where do you go for a breath of fresh air when you are surrounded by pollutants? Air pollution is any chemical in the air that can cause harm to people or other living things. Some common pollutants are smoke, carbon monoxide, nitrogen dioxide, sulfur dioxide, ozone, and lead. Many cause direct harm when animals breathe them or take them in through their skin. Others mix with harmless chemicals in the atmosphere to form acid rain or smog. Even chemicals that are not normally poisonous, such as carbon dioxide, can cause far-reaching environmental problems when given off in large amounts. People are working to reduce air pollution by using air filters and smokestack scrubbers in factories and power plants, and catalytic converters in cars. Alternative energy sources, environmentally friendly materials, and new production and disposal processes are also being developed. Governments are setting limits and charging fines to companies that produce pollution. International treaties, such as the Kyoto Protocol, organize the efforts of many countries together to reduce these harmful gases.

did you know?

A PERIOD OF EXTREME AIR POLLUTION IN LONDON, CALLED *THE GREAT SMOG OF 1952*, KILLED CLOSE TO 4,000 PEOPLE IN JUST 4 DAYS.

WHERE DOES IT COME FROM? ▼

Pollutants can come from natural and human sources. Smoke is produced during a forest fire. Volcanoes produce sulfur dioxide and carbon dioxide. Carbon monoxide, nitrogen oxides, and sulfur dioxide come from car exhaust and gases released from burning fuel in power plants. Lead can come from industrial wastes and cars, and ozone is created when other pollutants react together in the atmosphere.

Wind can carry air pollution hundreds of miles and affect communities far from its source.

Steel manufacturing is one source of air pollution in Volta Redonda, Brazil.

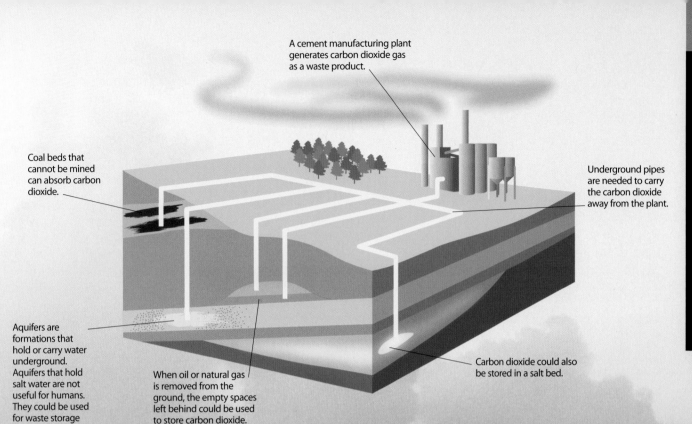

A cement manufacturing plant generates carbon dioxide gas as a waste product.

Coal beds that cannot be mined can absorb carbon dioxide.

Underground pipes are needed to carry the carbon dioxide away from the plant.

Aquifers are formations that hold or carry water underground. Aquifers that hold salt water are not useful for humans. They could be used for waste storage instead.

When oil or natural gas is removed from the ground, the empty spaces left behind could be used to store carbon dioxide.

Carbon dioxide could also be stored in a salt bed.

▲ REDUCING AIR POLLUTION

There are two main ways to lower the amount of air pollution created by humans. One is to produce less air pollution by using clean energy sources, such as wind or solar. The other is to reduce the amount of pollution released to the atmosphere by catching the pollutants. Carbon capture and storage (CCS) is a new technology that traps carbon dioxide gas and stores it underground. This process might help coal-fired plants minimize their carbon dioxide discharge, but it has its problems. The technology is expensive, and leakage into drinking water supplies or back into the atmosphere is a big concern.

Smokestacks carry the gas above the buildings. However, clouds of the pollutants quickly mix with the air surrounding the town.

ALGAE

Some may be tiny—living as microscopic, single cells in soil, on rocks, or in water. Others may be tall—making up dense underwater forests of seaweed 100 feet (about 30 m) high. Whether tiny or tall, algae are important organisms! Algae are producers. Producers are living things that make their own food from carbon dioxide and water, using the energy from sunlight. The oxygen made by algae helps living things all over the world survive. And, as producers, algae form the base of many aquatic food chains. They are especially important in ocean food chains. There, the algae living in the sunlit upper waters are food to countless other organisms. And those organisms are food for even larger organisms, and so on up the food chain. In this way, the energy of sunlight is transferred from one living thing to another throughout the ocean.

WALLS OF GLASS ▶

Diatoms may seem like tiny glass ornaments. In fact, they are microscopic algae that have cell walls made of silica, the main substance that makes up sand and glass. Most diatoms live as single cells in oceans, lakes, and soils. It is estimated that diatoms carry out more than a quarter of the world's photosynthesis.

Ocean diatom found near the island of Oahu, Hawaii

Diatoms can have a wide variety of shapes, including long rods, round discs, fat cylinders, and stars, such as this one.

did you know? GIANT KELPS ARE MANY-CELLED ALGAE THAT CAN GROW TO A LENGTH OF 200 FEET (60 M).

SUNLIGHT HARVESTERS ▼

Algae, such as this single-celled desmid, are like tiny solar panels. The broad, flat shapes of algae can maximize the amount of sunlight that they take in. They use sunlight to produce sugars and oxygen through the process of photosynthesis. Photosynthesis takes place in cell structures called *chloroplasts*. A pigment called *chlorophyll* found in chloroplasts gives many algae and plants their vivid green color.

Freshwater desmid

The nucleus of a desmid is located in the very center of the cell.

A desmid reproduces by splitting along this central line. A new half grows onto each of the original half cells.

◄ VISIBLE FROM SPACE

When conditions are right, algae can multiply quickly in a very short period of time. These quick population spurts are called *algal blooms*. Algae called *coccolithophores* live in ocean surface waters, where they can get enough light to carry out photosynthesis. They can sometimes form algal blooms so large that they can be seen from space.

From the space shuttle *Discovery*, trillions of single-celled algae look like a turquoise cloud swirling in the Atlantic Ocean.

ALLERGIES

After Jamie took a sip of Liza's drink, his throat swelled and he was rushed to the hospital. Six-month-old Kate was there because she had started wheezing. What was the culprit? Allergies. Liza had been eating peanuts, and Jamie, who is allergic to nuts, had experienced a severe allergic reaction to Liza's saliva on the cup. Kate's asthma was caused by her allergies to the pollens in the air. An allergy is a reaction by your immune system to something that does not bother most people. Allergens, the substances that cause allergies, are everywhere— pollens, foods, mold, dust mites, pets, even medicines—and about one in five people in the United States suffers from allergies. Some allergic reactions can be irritating, such as sneezing, hives, or watery eyes, but some can be deadly if they are not treated immediately.

DUST MITES ▶

Unlike this model, real dust mites can't be seen without magnification. Yet they can cause big allergy problems—sneezing, itching, watery eyes, stuffy ears, skin rashes, and even asthma. Dust mite feces and tiny pieces of their bodies get mixed in with dust. When the dust is disturbed, the particles can be inhaled. Achoo!

Dust mites are eight-legged creatures that are related to spiders.

Some mites' hairs may sense electrical signals.

Dust mites feed on dead skin cells that people shed.

Unmagnified, this flower pollen grain would look like a speck of dust. Allergies to pollen are sometimes called *hay fever*.

Pollen grains are transported by wind, water, or insects to fertilize other plants of the same species.

ASTHMA ►

This grass plant may look innocent enough, but to someone with asthma, it may say "danger." Asthma is a disease of the lungs that affects more than 17 million Americans. For most asthma sufferers, allergies play a part in causing the asthma or in making it worse. Pollens from this grass plant may cause airways to tighten, inducing coughing, wheezing, and shortness of breath.

If this pollen grain from the European field elm touches the lining of a hay fever sufferer's nose, the mucous membranes swell.

THE BATTLE ▲

Suppose you eat, touch, or breathe an allergen. If you have allergies, your white blood cells, which fight disease, make an antibody called *immunoglobulin E (IgE)*. IgE attaches to immune cells called *mast cells,* many of which are in your nose, eyes, lungs, and intestines. These cells become sensitized against another attack. If that happens, the mast cells release chemicals called *mediators*, which get more white blood cells to join the fight. Tissues swell, causing allergy misery. A sudden or large mediator release can cause a severe reaction. One well-known mediator is histamine, whose effects can be blocked by medicines called antihistamines.

 did you
know?..........................
ONLY EIGHT FOODS CAUSE 90 PERCENT OF FOOD ALLERGIES IN THE UNITED STATES.

ALS

Patients with ALS, or amyotrophic lateral sclerosis, may feel like prisoners in their own bodies. Yet, with help, some survive for decades to live very full lives. ALS is a disease that results from the gradual weakening of the nerves, called *motor neurons*, that control muscle movement. When the nerves stop working, the muscles they control get weaker and thinner. People with ALS slowly lose control of their arms, legs, and even the muscles that allow them to speak. They eventually become paralyzed. Thankfully, they usually keep their ability to think, sense, or understand the world around them. Scientists do not know what causes ALS. Some forms of the disease can be inherited. Viruses or environmental toxins may play a role as well. ALS is also known as Lou Gehrig's disease, after a famous American baseball player who had the disease.

LIFE WITH ALS ▲

Stephen Hawking, a famous British theoretical physicist, has lived with ALS for over 40 years. He was diagnosed when he was 21, after noticing that he had become clumsy. Over time, he became dependent on a wheelchair and had to use a speech synthesizer to speak. With help from his wife, children, nurses, assistants, and technology, he has written important research papers and best-selling books, given many lectures, appeared in movies and television, and has even been in space.

did you know?..........................
MOTOR NEURONS CAN BE MORE THAN 3 FEET LONG. THE LONGEST ONE RUNS FROM YOUR LOWER SPINE TO YOUR BIG TOE.

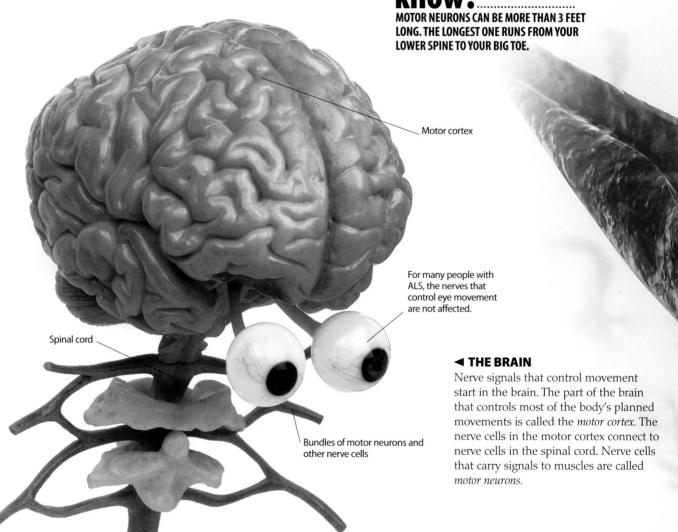

Motor cortex

For many people with ALS, the nerves that control eye movement are not affected.

Spinal cord

Bundles of motor neurons and other nerve cells

◄ THE BRAIN

Nerve signals that control movement start in the brain. The part of the brain that controls most of the body's planned movements is called the *motor cortex*. The nerve cells in the motor cortex connect to nerve cells in the spinal cord. Nerve cells that carry signals to muscles are called *motor neurons.*

▼ MOTOR NEURON

A motor neuron is made up of a cell body, several short arms called *dendrites*, and one long arm called an *axon*. The cell body and dendrites receive incoming signals. The axon sends out signals. A signal is a moving electrical charge that travels from cell to cell.

Direction of signal

❶ AXON

An axon carries a signal away from a neuron. In this model, the arms with knobby ends—such as the one numbered *1*—are the tips of axons from other neurons, carrying incoming signals to this motor neuron. The signal is traveling in the direction of the arrows.

❷ SYNAPSE

The place where the knobby end passes a signal to this motor neuron is called a *synapse*. The signal has to cross the gap at the synapse to get from one neuron to another.

❸ CELL BODY

The thickest part of the cell is called the *cell body,* where the nucleus is located. From there, the signal travels out on this neuron's axon to move a muscle.

❹ MYELIN

Flat cells wrap around axons the way a bandage is wrapped around a finger. They form a material called *myelin*. Myelin acts as the insulation in an electrical wire does, keeping nerve signals strong over long distances.

❺ DENDRITE

The spokelike dendrites deliver incoming signals from other nerve cells.

ALTITUDE

We live at the bottom of a deep sea—a sea of air. In an underwater sea, the pressure increases as you go deeper. In this sea of air, the pressure is also greatest at the bottom, where we live, and it decreases as you go higher. On Earth, altitude, or elevation, is measured from sea level. Sea level corresponds to the surface of the ocean between high and low tide. The city of New Orleans is located at about sea level, so its elevation is 0. Denver is about a mile (1,609 m) above sea level. In Denver, the air pressure is lower than at sea level, and this pressure difference can affect people and other living things. For example, athletes who train at sea level often have trouble performing their sport at higher altitudes. High altitudes offer many challenges.

If the instruments that keep an airplane cabin pressurized stop working, the air might not have enough oxygen for passengers to breathe comfortably.

When airplane cabin pressure is low, passengers can wear masks that deliver air mixed with oxygen.

LESS OXYGEN ▲

Lower air pressure means that there are fewer molecules in the same volume of air. This "thinner" air has fewer oxygen molecules than air at higher pressure. Because people need oxygen to survive, air with fewer oxygen molecules can cause physical stress to the body. For this reason, airplanes flying at high altitudes usually have pressurized cabins so the air pressure inside is similar to that on the ground.

did you know?
IN 1953, A MAN FROM NEPAL AND A MAN FROM NEW ZEALAND BECAME THE FIRST PEOPLE TO REACH THE SUMMIT OF MOUNT EVEREST.

▼ **SURVIVING HIGH ALTITUDE**

The highest place on Earth is the summit of Mt. Everest, with an elevation of about 29,035 feet (8,850 m). Adventurers who climb to this altitude face many dangers. One serious risk is altitude sickness, or acute mountain sickness (AMS). The low pressure and low levels of oxygen can cause dizziness, headaches, nausea, increased heart rate, and shortness of breath. To prevent AMS, mountain climbers must make their climbs slowly, so their bodies can adjust to the altitude.

Mountain climbers wear thick, down-filled suits to protect themselves from the freezing temperatures.

To help battle low oxygen conditions, mountain climbers often wear oxygen masks. These masks are attached to oxygen canisters and regulators that climbers keep in their backpacks.

AMAZON RIVER

The Amazon River practically cuts South America in half. It starts in the Andes Mountains, close to the Pacific Ocean, and flows almost 4,000 miles (6,400 km) across the continent to the Atlantic. For most of its length, the Amazon pushes lazily through the gentle slopes of the forest. Don't let that pace fool you, though. The Amazon carries more water than any river in the world. In some places it is so wide that you cannot see from one bank to the other. It carries trillions of gallons of water—more than ten times the flow of the Mississippi River. Even so, it has incredible force. When it reaches the Atlantic Ocean, the Amazon River's fresh water pushes the ocean's salt water for more than 100 miles (161 km) before they mix.

DRAINING A BASIN ▼

The Amazon River, and the rivers that feed into it, drain a vast area of South America. This area, called the Amazon basin, covers more than 2.7 million square miles (7 million sq km)—almost as much as the continental United States. The Amazon basin is home to thousands of species of animals. In the river, manatees munch on aquatic plants. Freshwater dolphins use the echoes of their high-pitched voices to find fish. Along the riverbank, you might find large hunters, such as the jaguar, the most powerful cat in the Americas.

One river cannot drain the basin by itself. More than 1,000 other rivers dump their waters into the Amazon, including the one shown here, the Tigre.

The Amazon is a river of many colors, from black to muddy yellow, depending on each region's soil and plants.

About 20 percent of the world's supply of fresh water flows down the Amazon River to the Atlantic Ocean.

THE TOP OF THE RIVER ▶

The waters of the Amazon and its tributaries aren't all calm and quiet. The river begins in the high mountains of Peru. As gravity pulls the water, it tumbles downward with amazing force, scouring rocks and carving deep canyons. The water pours over cliffs, creating crashing waterfalls, some of them hundreds of feet high. The sediments from the high river nourish the land far downstream. Don't try rafting here!

did you know?..................

ALTHOUGH THE AMAZON CUTS ALL THE WAY ACROSS BRAZIL, NOT A SINGLE BRIDGE CROSSES THE RIVER.

Between 60 and 140 inches (about 1,500–3,500 mm) of rain fall each year in the Amazon basin.

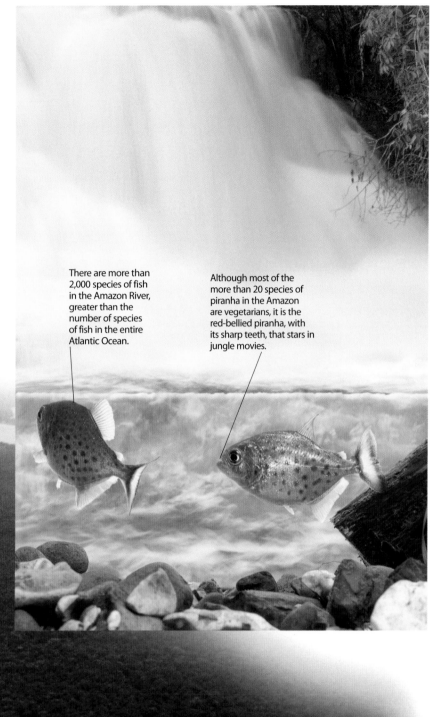

There are more than 2,000 species of fish in the Amazon River, greater than the number of species of fish in the entire Atlantic Ocean.

Although most of the more than 20 species of piranha in the Amazon are vegetarians, it is the red-bellied piranha, with its sharp teeth, that stars in jungle movies.

The rain forest creates its own rain. About half of the water vapor in the air comes from the leaves of plants.

ANIMAL BODIES

Porcupine spines, elephant trunks, and delicate butterfly wings. You can recognize many animals by the special structures, or parts, of their bodies. But these structures do more than just show who's who. They also help the animal survive. For example, an elephant's trunk is long, strong, and flexible, making it useful for grabbing food, collecting water, and interacting with other elephants. Animals' bodies are loaded with parts that help them stay alive. Take eyes, for example. Beavers have an inner eyelid that they can see through under water. A similar eyelid keeps sand out of camels' eyes. Frogs' eyeballs can sink back into their skulls to help push large prey down their throats.

A porcupine's spines are made out of the same protein that makes up hair and fingernails.

Mammals, such as porcupines and armadillos, have hair. This important structure helps them stay warm.

The bands on a nine-banded armadillo are joints that let the animal bend its body. Otherwise, its armor is not very flexible!

LITTLE ARMORED ONE ▼

Armadillos are the only mammals alive with such a hard, leathery shell. *Armadillo*, in fact, means "little armored one" in Spanish. This nine-banded armadillo is an insect-eating mammal about the size of a small cat. It lives in the southeastern United States. The armadillo's shell offers good protection from its enemies. When not hunting for food, the armadillo spends most of its time sleeping in an underground burrow.

▼ WATCH OUT! PORCUPINE SPINES!

The African porcupine is a large rodent whose back and tail are covered with long, sharp spines. When the porcupine is in danger, it raises its spines so it seems much bigger than it is. If a predator attacks anyhow—ouch! The spines pull off easily, leaving the predator with a painful reminder of how risky it is to try to eat a porcupine.

The claws help the spider hold its prey and its ground during a fight.

Near the fangs are *pedipalps* that help hold prey. In adult males, they hold sperm.

▼ DANGER! POISON!

Funnel-web spiders are large and extremely poisonous spiders found in Australia. They are mostly black, with a body size ranging from half an inch (1.5 cm) to almost two inches (5 cm) long. Fierce hunters, funnel-web spiders trap their prey in sock-shaped webs built in underground burrows. They are feared for their dangerous venom, even though they bite humans only in self-defense.

The fangs are strong and sharp enough to pierce through soft shoes—or fingernails!

This venom is among the most toxic in the world. A bite to a human causes extreme pain and can even cause death.

A spider uses its spinnerets to make silk for building webs.

Spiders have hard, shell-like armor instead of bones to give their bodies support and strength.

A tiny spur on the second leg shows that this is the male—smaller than the female, but with a much more toxic bite.

The spider's tiny hairs allow it to sense the movement of air when prey or predators come near.

did you know?..........................
A SURPRISED ARMADILLO CAN JUMP MORE THAN THREE FEET (1 M) STRAIGHT UP—4 TIMES ITS HEIGHT!

ANIMAL COMMUNICATION

Elephants trumpet. Bees dance. Animals communicate in many ways. Bees dance to describe the location of food to others. Bears rub and scratch trees to mark their territories. Cuttlefish and squid distract predators by changing color and flashing colorful splotches across their skin. Frogs, birds, and whales sing to attract mates. Acoustic signals are some of the most important means of communication. We can hear an enormous variety of squeaks, rumbles, hisses, and roars in the world around us. We cannot detect some sounds because their frequencies are too high or too low for our hearing. Often, animals use a mixture of sounds of different frequencies. For example, a mouse can alert other nearby mice of danger by using high-pitched sounds that the predator cannot hear. The lower-pitched mouse squeaks that we can hear travel farther, to give more distant warnings.

Penguin parents travel great distances for food. They call to locate their mate and chick when they return.

▼ DISTANT VIBRATIONS

Elephants often communicate with rumbling noises made in their throats and trunks. Some strong low-frequency rumbles can travel 6 miles (10 km) through the air. Elephants can also feel and interpret slight vibrations in the ground from even farther away. They sense the vibrations through their sensitive feet!

The trunk is used in social interactions such as play and courtship and for communicating with sound, smell, and touch.

Finding your chick in a colony of thousands is a challenge!

did you know? WHALES SENSE SOUND THROUGH FAT-FILLED CAVITIES IN THEIR LOWER JAW THAT TRANSMIT SIGNALS TO THE MIDDLE EAR.

HOW WILL I EVER FIND YOU? ▶

Penguin contact calls are individually identifiable, just like human voices. They allow mates and chicks to recognize each other easily, despite the loud background noise of the colony. Penguins also communicate with each other as they defend their territory and find mates. Once the female lays eggs, she and her mate have to keep finding each other so they can take turns sitting on the eggs and swimming off to eat. They do this with calls and displays, such as bowing, quivering, and head swinging.

ASTEROIDS

If you can imagine a rock the size of a city moving through space, you have a good idea of what an asteroid is. Asteroids are rocky objects that orbit the sun. Some are smaller than a house, but the largest is almost as wide as Texas. Most asteroids are in the asteroid belt between the orbits of Mars and Jupiter. The millions of asteroids there are probably left over from when the solar system formed. Some asteroids have orbits that extend past Neptune, the farthest planet. Others have orbits that bring them close to Earth. Astronomers watch for these asteroids because of the damage they could cause if they were to hit Earth. Fortunately, asteroids large enough to cause widespread destruction hit Earth only every thousand years or so.

▼ WHAT'S MISSING?

Notice something missing in this picture? Unlike most asteroids, which are covered with craters from their many collisions, Itokawa has no craters. No one knows exactly why, but one idea is that Itokawa's rocks are so loosely held together that collisions shake piles of rubble into the craters, filling in the holes.

▼ EXPLODING FAMILIES

Families aren't just for people. Most asteroids in the asteroid belt are members of families, too! Families are groups of asteroids with similar properties and orbits. The steps below show how an asteroid family forms.

1 A stray asteroid or other object moves through the solar system on a collision course with an asteroid. The asteroid it hits is called the *parent asteroid*.

2 Before the collision, the parent asteroid is in orbit within the asteroid belt.

3 When the object crashes into the parent asteroid, its energy is transferred to the spot where the object hits.

4 The parent asteroid explodes into smaller pieces. Each piece has the same chemical makeup as the parent asteroid.

▲ BAKED IN SPACE?

Ida was named for a Greek nymph, not for its resemblance to an Idaho potato. Ida is about 37 miles (60 km) wide. You can tell from the number of craters that Ida is held together more strongly than Itokawa is. Ida is different from most asteroids because it has a moon! Ida's moon is less than a mile (1.5 km) wide. This moon, Dactyl, was the first ever discovered orbiting an asteroid.

CERES—A ROUND ASTEROID ▼

Have you ever wondered why planets are round? Ceres—the largest asteroid in the asteroid belt—reveals the answer. In order for an object in space to be round, it must have enough mass that its own gravity pulls it into a round shape. Ceres is about 600 miles (960 km) wide. Its mass is great enough to pull it into a ball. Also like the planets, Ceres has layers—a core, a mantle, and a crust.

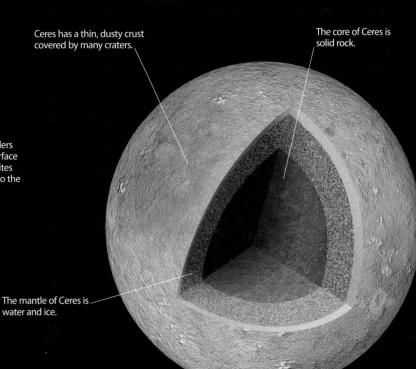

Ceres has a thin, dusty crust covered by many craters.

The core of Ceres is solid rock.

The giant boulders on Itokawa's surface may be meteorites that crashed into the asteroid.

The mantle of Ceres is water and ice.

Over time, the gravitational pulls of Mars and Jupiter cause the pieces of the new asteroid family to settle into orbits that are similar to one another.

ASTRONAUTS

Drinking balls of floating fruit juice may be fun, but astronauts can also have it tough, especially when they suffer from "puffy-head bird-leg syndrome"! Living in microgravity—that is, almost no gravity—the fluid that is usually pulled down into the astronauts' legs stays in their face, chest, and arms. That gives them a puffy face and skinny legs, at least until the flight is done. In space, human bodies have to adjust to microgravity so that they can maintain homeostasis. Homeostasis is the condition in which the human body's internal environment is kept stable in spite of change in the outside environment. Our bodies have systems that help us stay in balance by taking in nutrients and getting rid of wastes. We breathe in oxygen and breathe out carbon dioxide. On a space shuttle or space station, maintaining homeostasis can be tricky, but training and technology have made it possible.

FOOD GOES IN ▶

Astronauts begin their meals with a pair of scissors, to cut open their airtight packages of food. Meals must, of course, contain all the nutrients that the astronauts need. But the meals also must be tidy. Food cannot be crumbly and create a mess that floats in the air—a danger to lungs and to equipment. And trash is carefully cleaned up, so there are no stray wrappers floating around.

Sweet and sour beef

Chunky chicken stew

Trail mix

Pineapple

Granola

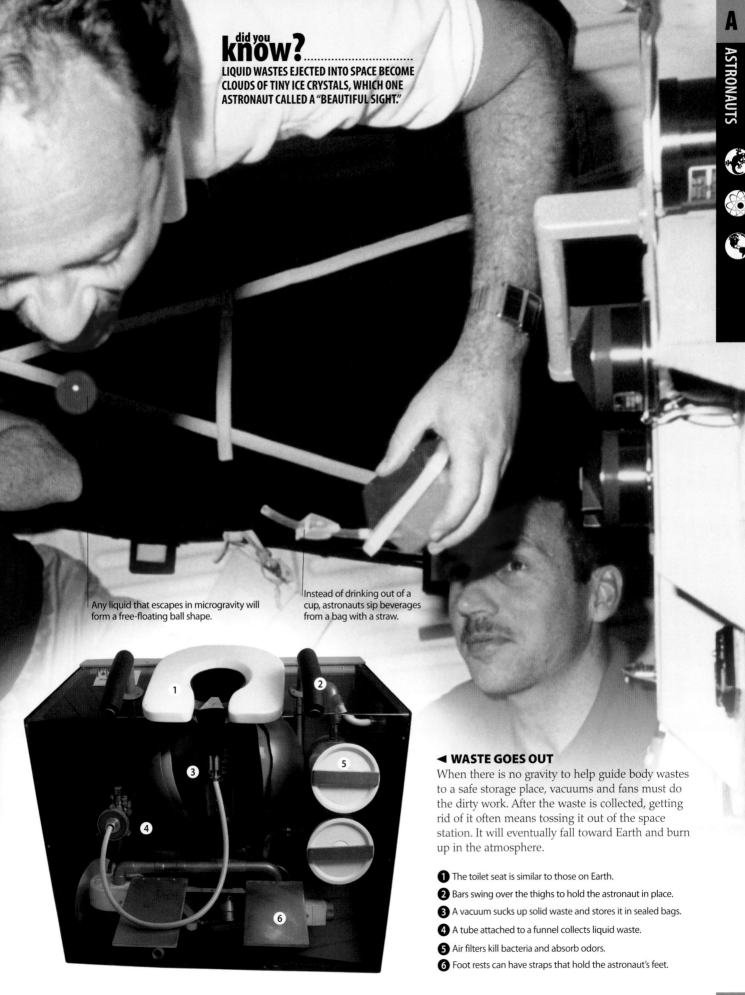

did you
know?.........................
LIQUID WASTES EJECTED INTO SPACE BECOME
CLOUDS OF TINY ICE CRYSTALS, WHICH ONE
ASTRONAUT CALLED A "BEAUTIFUL SIGHT."

Any liquid that escapes in microgravity will
form a free-floating ball shape.

Instead of drinking out of a
cup, astronauts sip beverages
from a bag with a straw.

◄ WASTE GOES OUT

When there is no gravity to help guide body wastes
to a safe storage place, vacuums and fans must do
the dirty work. After the waste is collected, getting
rid of it often means tossing it out of the space
station. It will eventually fall toward Earth and burn
up in the atmosphere.

❶ The toilet seat is similar to those on Earth.

❷ Bars swing over the thighs to hold the astronaut in place.

❸ A vacuum sucks up solid waste and stores it in sealed bags.

❹ A tube attached to a funnel collects liquid waste.

❺ Air filters kill bacteria and absorb odors.

❻ Foot rests can have straps that hold the astronaut's feet.

ASTRONOMY MYTHS

Have you ever wished on a falling star? A falling star is really just a meteor, but according to myth, a falling star can make your wish come true! Long before scientists knew about meteors, planets, and stars, people looked up at the night sky and wondered about the lights they saw there. Ancient astronomers noticed that most of the lights twinkled and moved in a predictable way. Other lights did not twinkle and seemed to wander in the sky. What were these lights, and why did they move? For many ancient people, the planets were gods or goddesses. Their movement might predict who would rise to power. Myths helped people try to make sense of the universe. A red sunset was the blood of the dying sun god. When the moon was not visible, a monster had eaten it.

EARTH IS THE CENTER ▶

Around 350 B.C., the philosopher Aristotle said that the planets moved on transparent crystal spheres that surrounded Earth. This geocentric, or Earth-centered, view of the universe lasted until the sixteenth century. Astronomer Nicolaus Copernicus revolutionized science when he stated that this idea was wrong. The sun—not Earth—is at the center of our solar system. The planets sometimes seem brighter and sometimes seem to move backward because our view of them changes as they move around the sun.

did you know?..............................
TEMPLES AND PYRAMIDS OF ANCIENT EGYPT WERE OFTEN BUILT FACING NORTH SO THAT THE KINGS COULD BECOME STARS IN THE NORTHERN

◄ WARRIORS IN THE SKY

Some of the greatest myths of ancient times were about constellations—groups of stars that looked like people or animals. For example, the group of stars we now call the Big Dipper was described in one myth as seven oxen. A nearby group of stars, known as Bootes, was a farmer who took care of the oxen. Myths often described the constellations as gods or great warriors.

An ancient Greek myth described the sun as the god Helios driving a chariot across the sky. Today, we know that the sun is a star that is so big, 1.3 million Earths could fit inside of it.

▲ A FLAT EARTH

Even back in Aristotle's day, people knew that Earth was round. Most historians agree that Christopher Columbus knew quite well that he would not sail off the edge of the Earth. Despite this, over the years, people developed myths about a flat Earth. The drawing above represents one artist's view of sailing across a flat Earth.

ATACAMA DESERT

The driest place on Earth is right next to the Pacific Ocean. It's the Atacama Desert, a narrow plateau that stretches more than 620 miles (1,000 km) along the coast of Chile. In some parts of the Atacama, rain has never been recorded! This is because the desert is bordered on the east by the high Andes Mountains and on the west by a coastal mountain range. The Andes block warm, wet air from reaching the desert. The air rises when it hits the mountains, cools, and then falls as snow in the mountains and rain in the Amazon rain forest. By the time the air reaches the Atacama Desert, it is dry. The air that blows in from the cold Pacific is dry, too.

SPINY SURVIVORS ▶

Although the Atacama's climate is extremely dry, a few plants have adapted to desert life. Many are unique to the region. Cactuses are some of the few organisms that can live in the Atacama's harsh conditions. Their stems are covered in a waxy coating that keeps the plant from losing too much water through its pores. Cactus roots are also close to the soil surface, so they can quickly suck up rain when it finally falls.

◀ A MOONSCAPE

Because it rarely rains in the Atacama, the soil is not moist enough to support much plant life. Few animals can survive here because there is little to eat. In fact, in the Atacama it rains on average only .004 inches (.01 cm) a year. By comparison, New Orleans receives an average of 58 inches (147 cm) of rain per year. Many parts of the Atacama are so barren, or lifeless, that they are often compared to the surface of the moon or Mars. NASA scientists found so little life in Atacama's soil that they suggested it would be a good place to test the equipment they use when they search for life on Mars.

This candelabra cactus grows less than 1/4 inch (5 mm) annually, about the length of an eyelash!

The air in the Atacama is so dry that clouds here are rare. The most significant source of moisture to the Atacama Desert is fog from the Pacific Ocean.

Unlike hot deserts such as the Sahara, the Atacama is relatively cool. Average daily temperatures range from 32°F to 77°F (0°C–25°C).

Human remains that are 9,000 years old have been found in the Atacama Desert. The dry air slows decomposition and keeps the mummies extremely well preserved.

did you know?
THE DRIEST PLACE ON EARTH IS JUST WEST OF ONE OF THE WETTEST PLACES ON EARTH—THE AMAZON BASIN.

Earth's atmosphere has a big job. It's like bubble wrap, protecting the planet and the life on it from the harsh conditions of space. It filters out dangerous radiation, stops meteors, and helps transfer heat across the globe. Billions of years ago, volcanoes belched out gases such as carbon dioxide, nitrogen, and water vapor. Some of those gases were held in by Earth's gravity. Many biochemical processes—cloud formation, rain, rock formation, and photosynthesis—eventually added oxygen to the mix. Now oxygen makes up 21 percent of the atmosphere. Oxygen, nitrogen, and traces of carbon dioxide and water vapor form an atmosphere that provides the materials for sustaining life on Earth.

UP TO THIN AIR

The layers of the atmosphere differ from one another in the number of gas particles they contain. The closer a layer is to Earth, the denser it is, because more gas particles are held by gravity. The troposphere and the stratosphere, together extending just 30 miles (50 km) above Earth's surface, contain 99 percent of the gases in the atmosphere. The air becomes increasingly thinner in the mesosphere, thermosphere, and exosphere.

The lower atmosphere holds most of the world's water vapor, giving rise to clouds and severe storms.

Thunderstorms can send special lightning—red rings, called *sprites*, and blue streaks, called *blue jets*—into the upper atmosphere.

HOT OR COLD UP THERE?

Each of the first three layers of the atmosphere is topped by an area called a *pause*, where temperatures change. As you climb to the tropopause, the top of the troposphere, the temperature drops to -60°F (-51°C). The stratosphere warms with altitude, to about 5°F (-15°C), as ozone forms a layer that absorbs the sun's UV radiation. The mesosphere has few particles to absorb solar radiation. It gets colder as you go up, reaching -184°F (-120°C). The thermosphere has even fewer particles, but they are closer to the sun and can heat up to 3,600°F (2,000°C).

did you know? SCORCHING PARTICLES IN THE THERMOSPHERE ARE SO FAR APART THAT THE AIR FEELS COOL. ....

Exosphere, where satellites orbit and Earth's atmosphere merges into space

Upper thermosphere, where air is so thin that it is often considered part of outer space

Lower thermosphere, where the space shuttle flies and auroras happen

Mesosphere, where most meteors burn up as shooting stars

Stratosphere, where commercial jets fly in the stable air layers

Troposphere, where most weather forms and small airplanes fly

Land and sea surfaces interact with the atmosphere.

Bedrock within Earth's crust separates magma from the surface.

High-energy gases dissolved in magma can help eject dust from erupting volcanoes even into Earth's stratosphere.

AURORA BOREALIS

You see a strange, glowing light in the corner of the night sky. The mysterious light grows into a swirling cloud of green and red that fills the sky above. Then, within hours, it fades back into darkness. You have just seen an aurora! An aurora is a natural light display seen at night in the polar regions of Earth. Auroras happen when charged particles from the sun reach the magnetic field that surrounds Earth and are trapped. Many of these trapped particles move toward Earth's magnetic poles. There, they can run into gas molecules in the atmosphere. These collisions give off light energy, producing an aurora. In the Northern Hemisphere these strange and beautiful lights are called the *aurora borealis,* or the northern lights. In the Southern Hemisphere, they are called the *aurora australis,* or the southern lights.

NORTHERN LIGHTS ▶
Most auroras occur about 60 miles (100 km) above Earth, in the thermosphere layer of the atmosphere, though they can occur 10 times higher. Auroras can have many different colors of light, caused by the different types of gas molecules in the atmosphere. Oxygen most often makes green light, the most common color of an aurora. Blue light is given off when the charged particles collide with nitrogen. Some of the light given off is ultraviolet light, which we cannot see.

did you
know?
THE COLLISIONS THAT CAUSE AURORAS ALSO TAKE PLACE DURING THE DAYTIME, BUT THEY ARE NOT BRIGHT ENOUGH TO BE SEEN.

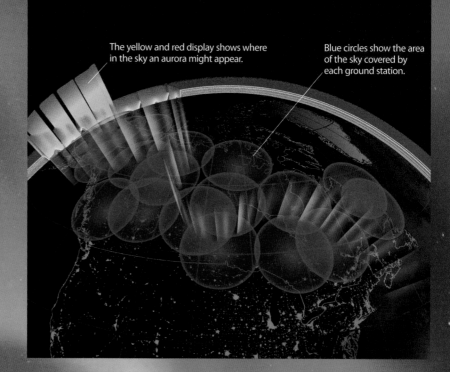

The yellow and red display shows where in the sky an aurora might appear.

Blue circles show the area of the sky covered by each ground station.

Aurora lights that occur very high in the sky can appear red or purple.

TRACKING AURORAS ▲

Sometimes an aurora will brighten, break up into smaller parts, and dance across the sky as it changes color. The cause of this special type of dancing aurora is unknown. To solve this mystery, NASA scientists will use data from probes launched into space and cameras on the ground. This image shows how the ground stations might detect an aurora.

Aurora borealis makes the sky appear green in Manitoba, Canada.

Some aurora displays can spread thousands of miles across the sky.

BACTERIA

When people say bacteria are everywhere, they really mean *everywhere!* Many bacteria are what's called *extremophiles.* An extremophile is a living thing that can survive under severe conditions. The Greek root *-phil-* means love, and these organisms love extreme places. Some bacteria are acidophiles, which means they live in acids. Other bacteria are halophiles and need to live in very salty water—so salty that it would kill most other living things. Xerophiles include bacteria that can live in rocks and soils that have very little water. Some bacteria—called *psychrophiles*—can even endure freezing temperatures. They live in polar ice caps. Because of the many different ways that they can survive, bacteria live in practically every environment on Earth. Scientists study extremophiles to see how life might form on other planets, where conditions are extreme.

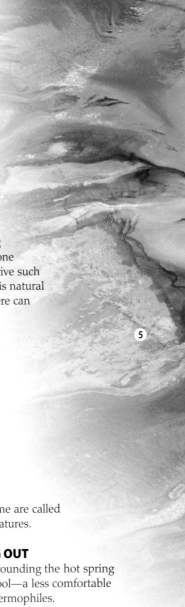

HOT STUFF ▶

Some like it hot—some bacteria that is. Water heated by melted rock deep underground reaches skin-burning temperatures in the Grand Prismatic Spring in Yellowstone National Park in Wyoming. Most organisms cannot survive such heat, but thermophiles—heat-loving bacteria—make this natural hot spring their home. The colorful bacteria that live there can survive in water as hot as 167°F (75°C).

❶ HEATED GROUNDWATER

The mineral water at the deepest center of the hot spring is 188°F (87°C). No life can survive here.

❷ COOLING OFF

Water in the shallower parts of the hot spring has been cooled slightly by the surrounding air. Bacteria that are green in color can survive the cooler temperatures.

❸ COOL AND COLORFUL

The bacteria that form the green, brown, and yellow slime are called *cyanobacteria.* They are yellow-green in warmer temperatures.

❹ NOT SO HOT

As waters cool near the edge of the hot spring, the cyanobacteria become orange and yellow. The color pigments produced by the bacteria act as a sunscreen.

❺ DRYING OUT

The soil surrounding the hot spring is dry and cool—a less comfortable home for thermophiles.

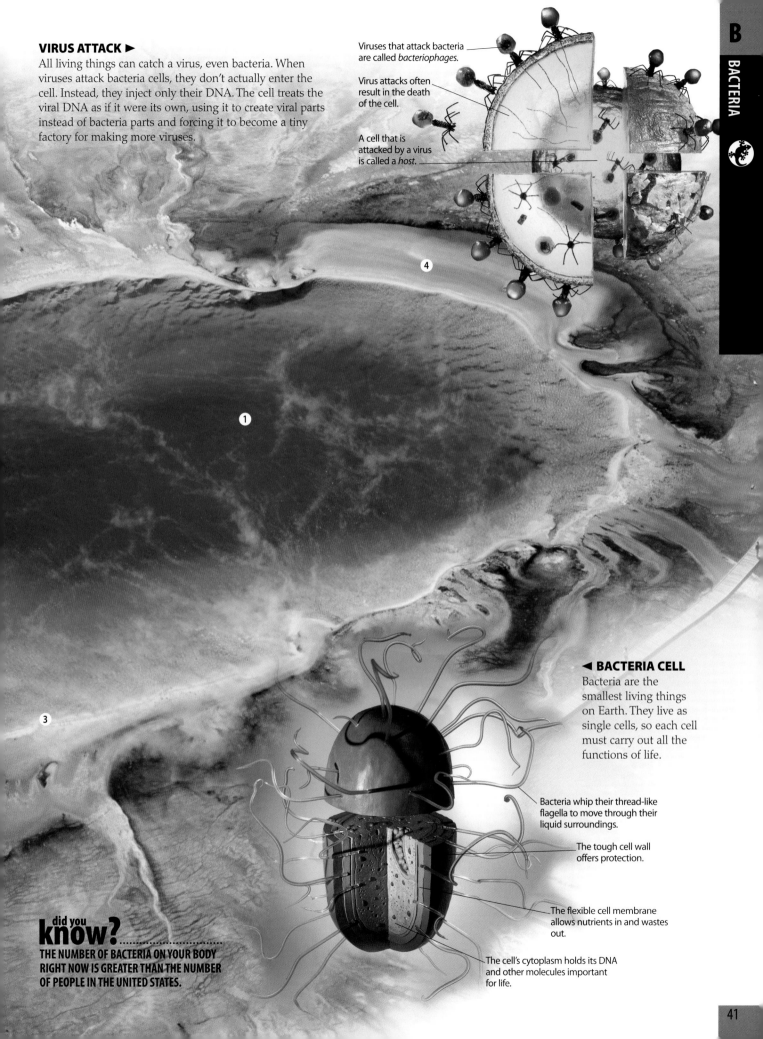

VIRUS ATTACK ▶

All living things can catch a virus, even bacteria. When viruses attack bacteria cells, they don't actually enter the cell. Instead, they inject only their DNA. The cell treats the viral DNA as if it were its own, using it to create viral parts instead of bacteria parts and forcing it to become a tiny factory for making more viruses.

Viruses that attack bacteria are called *bacteriophages.*

Virus attacks often result in the death of the cell.

A cell that is attacked by a virus is called a *host.*

◀ BACTERIA CELL

Bacteria are the smallest living things on Earth. They live as single cells, so each cell must carry out all the functions of life.

Bacteria whip their thread-like flagella to move through their liquid surroundings.

The tough cell wall offers protection.

The flexible cell membrane allows nutrients in and wastes out.

The cell's cytoplasm holds its DNA and other molecules important for life.

did you know?................
THE NUMBER OF BACTERIA ON YOUR BODY RIGHT NOW IS GREATER THAN THE NUMBER OF PEOPLE IN THE UNITED STATES.

BARRACUDA

Barracudas have earned the nickname "Tiger of the Sea" because of their hunting prowess. You have to look only once at their ferocious mouths to realize why they are such good hunters, and why they've been successful for 50 million years. Barracudas are found worldwide in tropical and subtropical ocean waters. Their long, thin bodies are flexible enough to maneuver through the twists and turns of coral reefs, where they are often found. A barracuda moves up and down quickly by inflating or deflating its swim bladder, a gas-filled chamber that changes the buoyancy of the fish. Like other fish, a barracuda is ectothermic, that is, its body temperature is determined by its environment. It is a vertebrate, has scales, and uses its gills to remove oxygen from the water to breathe.

OPEN WIDE! ▼
Barracudas can open their mouths extremely wide to capture large fish. Barracudas are ambush feeders. They rest quietly until they spot prey, and then charge suddenly—up to 36 miles per hour (58 km/h)! Their long teeth fit into holes in the other side of their jaw. This allows the barracuda to close its mouth on captured prey, slicing the fish in half.

Barracudas have no eyelids, so they never close their eyes. Instead of sleeping, they swim slowly at night in a trancelike state.

did you know?
BARRACUDAS ARE ATTRACTED TO SHINY THINGS THAT GLINT LIKE SILVERY FISH, SO DIVERS ARE SMART TO LEAVE JEWELRY, WATCHES, AND METAL OBJECTS AT HOME!

Barracudas have two rows of teeth. Small, razor-sharp teeth grow on the outside of the jaw. Large fanglike teeth grow inside the smaller teeth.

TOXIC FISH ▶
There are 26 known species of barracuda, some of which can grow up to six feet (1.83 m) long. Barracudas eat all types of fish, from tiny anchovies to much larger fish like tuna. Because they are at the top of the food chain, barracudas accumulate toxins from the fish they eat. People who eat barracuda may get a serious illness called *ciguatera poisoning,* which can last for weeks or months.

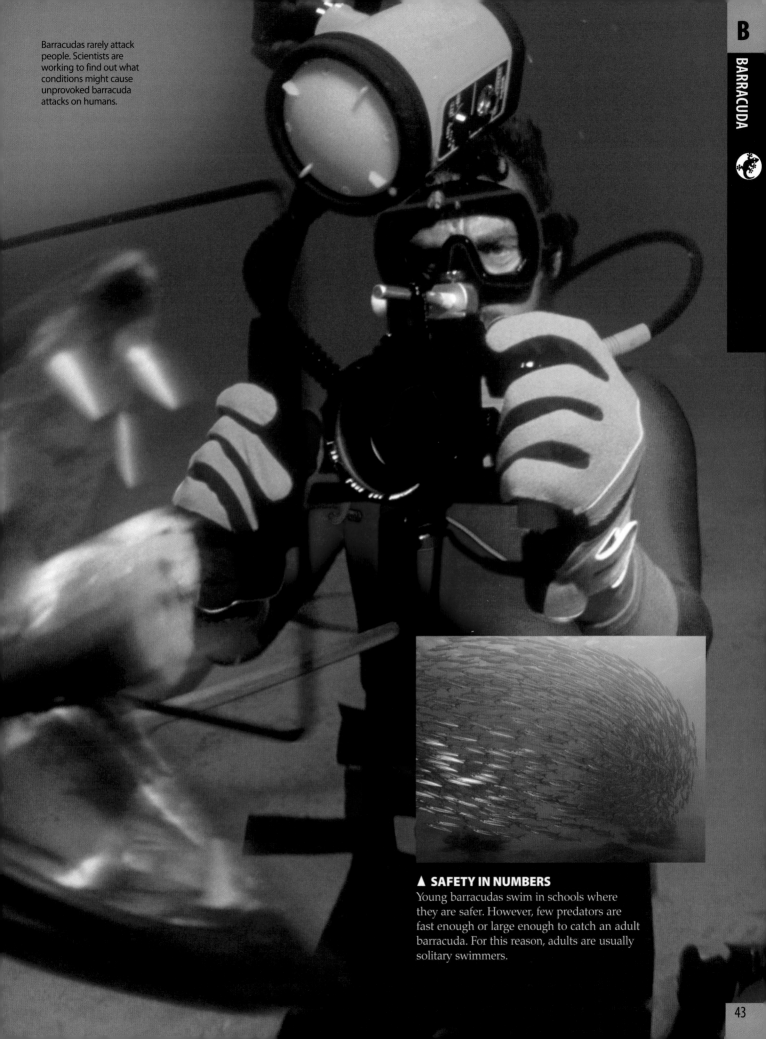

Barracudas rarely attack people. Scientists are working to find out what conditions might cause unprovoked barracuda attacks on humans.

▲ SAFETY IN NUMBERS

Young barracudas swim in schools where they are safer. However, few predators are fast enough or large enough to catch an adult barracuda. For this reason, adults are usually solitary swimmers.

BATS

"I vant to suck your blood." This line is a familiar one in old vampire movies. Though vampires are fictional characters, vampire bats are real. You won't find vampire bats sucking your blood, however. They rarely bite humans. Actually, they don't really bite at all. They make an incision with their sharp teeth and lick the blood as it oozes out. There are approximately 925 species of bats, few of them vampire bats. Bats are found around the world, with the greatest number of species in the tropics. Wherever they live, bats are an important link in ecosystems and benefit people much more than they harm them.

Bats are completely relaxed when hanging upside down.

Bats are the only mammals that can fly.

BATS AND BUGS ▶

If mosquitoes are a problem where you live, you know they are worst at dusk. This is when bats come out to feed. These Mexican freetail bats are part of the Bracken Creek Cave Colony in Texas. The more than 20 million bats in the colony can consume 250 tons of insects in one night! That's a lot of mosquitoes!

◀ BATS AND PLANTS

Bananas, anyone? Fruit bats, such as this one, pollinate banana plants. In fact, bats pollinate more than 400 species of plants. Fruit bats digest seeds and disperse them in their guano (poop). Guano is quite useful. Beetles eat it and humans use it as fertilizer.

Bat wings are actually skin membranes.

Long ears fold when the bats rest.

BAT HABITATS

Many bats, such as those in the enormous colony shown here, live in caves, but some bats have had to get creative after their habitats were lost due to urban development. The grey long-eared bat often lives in tunnels or buildings with crevices. The largest urban colony of bats in the world roosts under a bridge in Austin, Texas. Now transportation departments look for ways to create more bat habitats because bats in an ecosystem provide great benefits, such as fewer mosquitoes and more bananas.

did you know? THE GUANO IN BRACKEN CAVE MAY BE AS DEEP AS 65 FEET (20 M).

BAY OF FUNDY

The tide is coming in. No problem—you're up on some rocks, 20 feet (6 m) above the beach. In most places, you'd stay dry, but not in the Bay of Fundy. When the tide roars in there, your perch could end up 30 feet (9 m) under water. The bay gets narrow, like a funnel, so water rises up its deep, steep sides. Also, the water has a long trip up the bay, so incoming and outgoing water overlap. This combination results in some of the highest tides in the world, over 50 feet (15 m). More than 100 billion tons of water rush in and out twice a day. Rivers that normally pour into the bay reverse flow and move violently backward as the tide rises. Rapids in the rivers tumble in one direction at low tide and in the other direction at high tide.

RIDING HIGH ▼
To get to the Bay of Fundy, follow the Atlantic coast of the United States north to Maine. Just before you cross into Canada, you will be at the mouth of the bay. Travel about 180 miles (290 km) northeast up the bay, and you will be at Minas Basin, which you see below at high tide, and on the opposite page at low tide.

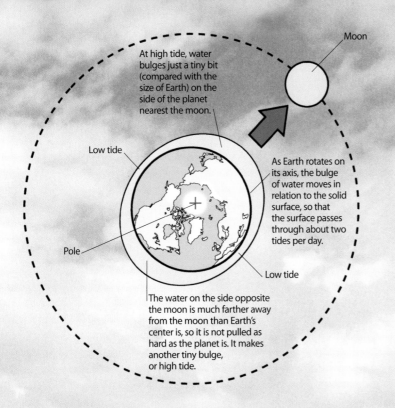

At high tide, water bulges just a tiny bit (compared with the size of Earth) on the side of the planet nearest the moon.

Moon

Low tide

Pole

As Earth rotates on its axis, the bulge of water moves in relation to the solid surface, so that the surface passes through about two tides per day.

Low tide

The water on the side opposite the moon is much farther away from the moon than Earth's center is, so it is not pulled as hard as the planet is. It makes another tiny bulge, or high tide.

◄ WHAT CAUSES TIDES?

The pull of gravity between the moon and Earth causes tides. The moon's tug is strongest on the side of Earth closest to it. Because water flows more easily than rock, the water on the moon side of Earth flows toward the moon and makes a bulge—that's high tide. But why is there a high tide on the opposite side of Earth at the same time? The moon pulls harder on the whole planet than it does on the water farthest away from it, and this difference leaves a bulge of water over on that opposite side as well!

did you know?..........................
A NATIVE AMERICAN LEGEND SAYS THAT THE GREAT TIDES OF THE BAY OF FUNDY ARE CAUSED BY A GIANT WHALE'S TAIL.

SCRAPING BOTTOM ▼
Twice a day, tides rush out of the bay, leaving behind a rich layer of nutrients in the mud. The mud flats teem with crustaceans, shellfish, and thousands of birds who feast on them. Plankton soak up the sun. The tides churn these plankton out into the bay, where humpback, minke, and right whales feed on them.

High tide line

BEACHES

Ah, the beach—sand, surf, and tropical sun. Or, icy waves, whipping winds, and slippery rocks! Beaches are not just in the tropics and are not always sandy. A beach is made of loose sediment particles that collect on shore, and they can be pebbly, rocky, or sandy. Beaches are part of a larger area called the intertidal zone. This is the area of shore and sea floor that exists between the high and low water marks. Creatures in this zone have it rough. They are submerged at high tide and exposed at low tide. The crabs, barnacles, and sea stars that live in this zone have to endure a wide range of conditions including rough waves, temperature extremes, and attacks from both marine and land predators. What a life!

PEBBLE BEACHES

Pebbly beaches, called *shingle* beaches, are common along the coast of Britain. Generally, the pebbles range in size from 1/12 inch to 8 inches (2 to 200 mm) in diameter. Shingle beaches tend to be steeper than sandy ones. When the waves return to the ocean—called *backwash*—they take more of the lighter particles of sand with them and leave more of the heavier pebbles behind, building up the beach.

Waves cause pebbles to crash into each other and wear down any rough edges.

Bivalves, such as scallops and clams, have two shells that are hinged together.

48

Gastropods, such as snails, live in the spirals inside these cone shells.

did you know?...................
BRAZIL, AUSTRALIA, AND BANGLADESH ARE JUST THREE OF THE COUNTRIES CLAIMING TO HAVE THE WORLD'S LONGEST BEACH.

ROCKY BEACHES

The coasts of Oregon and Washington are famous for their beautiful rocky beaches, steep cliffs, and tidal pools. Tidal pools are hollows in the rocks that fill up with water at high tide. These pools are full of life—much of it attached to the rocks.

Sea stars, hermit crabs, anemones, and barnacles have all adapted to life in tidal pools. Tides refill the pools twice daily, which keeps the animals from drying out.

SANDY BEACHES

White sand beaches such as this one in Hawaii are made of tiny bits of broken coral and crushed shells. Most sand, though, comes from the weathering of inland rocks. Wind, rivers, and waves deposit the sand on the beach. Sandy beaches can be green, black, and even pink, depending on the rock they came from. Shells such as the ones above often wash up unbroken on a sandy beach.

BEARS

With their large furry bodies, short legs, and short tails, bears may appear clumsy. But don't let appearances fool you. They can run up to 30 miles per hour (48 km/h) and can climb and swim well, too. Bears have had a lot of time to practice, though. They have been around for 40 million years. The brown bear and the American black bear evolved from ancient bears. The grizzly bear is a type of brown bear found only in North America. Today bears live in many habitats around the world, and wherever they live, they have adapted to their surroundings. Brown bears live in forests, tundra, and mountain regions. Black bears prefer thick forests. Despite their reputations as carnivores, bears eat mostly plants. They are solitary creatures, and can roam great distances, traveling to wherever food is most plentiful at each time of the year. They have a keen sense of direction. Bears can find their way hundreds of miles to a food supply remembered from previous years.

NO FOOD OR WATER FOR MONTHS ▶

Brown bears are the some of the largest bears, and they will make good use of their extra weight. In fall or winter, many bears crawl into a small den and sleep for two to seven months without eating, drinking, or passing wastes —a phase called *hibernation*. The bear's heart rate slows, and its body temperature drops. It breathes slowly because it requires less oxygen when at rest. During hibernation, fat tissues break down to supply all the water and calories bears need.

Bears can smell food under several feet of snow! They can sniff out ripe berries, honey, or salmon from miles away!

FEEDING FRENZY ▲

Bears must gain enormous amounts of weight so they can survive the winter when food is scarce. In the summer and fall, bears go into a feeding frenzy, eating high-calorie foods such as fish, nuts, and fruit. Some bears gain 30 pounds (14 kg) per week and eat 20 hours per day!

BEAR CUBS ▶

Bears do not have many offspring. Black bears will have around 14 descendants in ten years during times when food is plentiful. Brown bears reproduce even more slowly. By comparison, a white-tailed deer might have 1,400 descendants in ten years.

Black bears' teeth are specially adapted for their diet. They have small cutting teeth common to carnivores, and flat molars to help them crush and chew plants.

Black bear claws are dark, short, and hooked to help climb trees. Unlike cats, bears cannot retract their claws.

Tiny newborn bear cubs gain weight fast. At 4 or 5 months, they weigh about 8 pounds (3.6 kg).

did you know? ALTHOUGH BEARS ARE LARGE, THEY GIVE BIRTH TO BABIES THAT WEIGH ONLY ABOUT A POUND (0.5 KG).

Brown bears can be identified by the hump on their backs, formed by large muscles that make the forelegs strong and powerful.

The long claws of a brown bear look as if they are made to tear meat, but they are used mostly for digging roots and grubs and for making dens.

BICYCLES

You've got a mile to travel and you're late! Would you rather walk or bicycle? If you want to save both your time and your energy, you'll take the bike. Why? Biking is more efficient than walking, because you travel farther with each "step." Using a simple machine known as the wheel and axle, a bicycle transfers the power of your legs into miles of rolling motion. That's why bicycles are used all over the world to deliver so many things, from mail to fresh-baked bread—even critical blood supplies through city traffic.

WHEEL TO WHEEL ▼

An axle is the bar in the middle of a wheel. When an axle is attached to a wheel, the two turn together. Turning the axle in a small circle also turns the wheel in a bigger circle. On a bike, the pedals are attached to an axle that turns one of the big toothy rings at your feet—called *chain rings*. The chain hooks onto those teeth and carries the force from your pedaling to the rear axle and wheel.

Mountain bike tires are thick. They grip difficult terrain better than thinner tires.

Pedal

The axle that the pedals turn is inside this.

Sprockets that attach to rear axle

Chain rings

Rear wheel's axle

Front wheel's axle

Chain

Rear axle attaches to the wheel here.

The rear derailleur moves the chain between sprockets.

THE EVOLUTION OF THE BICYCLE ▼

Some early bicycles had gigantic front wheels. The pedals were attached to the axle of the front wheel, as they are on a tricycle, so a bigger wheel went farther. A bicycle that uses a chain doesn't need that big front wheel, because the power from the wheel and axle at the pedals is multiplied by the power from the rear wheel and axle. Various sized chain rings and sprockets on the back wheel let riders change gears to match the terrain. Other changes to bikes have made them even more efficient. Early bikes weighed as much as 80 pounds (36 kg). Some road bikes now weigh as little as 20 pounds (9 kg). The International Cycling Union requires racers to use bikes that weigh at least 6.8 kilograms (about 15 lb), so that racers won't have an unfair advantage with an even lighter bicycle. Skinny tires reduce friction—all in all, more power for the pedal!

did you
know?.........................

IN A YEAR, CHINA MAKES MORE BICYCLES THAN ALL THE AUTOMOBILES MADE WORLDWIDE.

Helmets can prevent up to 88 percent of cyclists' brain injuries—extra important when riding through trees!

Elbow guards protect you from cuts and scrapes. They can even keep you from breaking your arm.

Gloves absorb shock, making your hands a lot more comfortable.

BIG BANG THEORY

We know that the universe is huge . . . and old . . . but how huge and old is it? And, how did it form? Scientists use mathematics to test ideas about just how the universe came to be what it is today. The idea that is accepted by most scientists is called the *big bang theory*. The big bang theory states that the universe began as an infinitely small point. This point contained all of the matter and energy in the universe today. Suddenly, a huge expansion occurred, called the *big bang*. As it expanded, the universe cooled and its matter spread far apart. It is still enlarging today. Scientists have found evidence of the big bang theory by studying galaxies. They found that the farther a galaxy is from Earth, the faster it is moving away from Earth. This can be true only if the universe is expanding in all directions.

TIMELINE OF THE UNIVERSE

This model shows how the universe formed 13.7 billion years ago. It shows the development from a tiny point to the 93-billion-light-years-wide observable cosmos that it is today. Keep in mind that the sizes, distances, and times shown here are not to scale. The universe is so large and so old that it would be impossible to fit its history onto the pages of a book.

At the big bang, the universe is extremely small, bright, dense, and hot.

Radiation fills the universe.

Less than a second after the big bang, the temperature is 10 million trillion degrees Celsius. Simple particles form.

Not quite 2 minutes after the big bang, the

did you know?.................

ASTRONOMERS ONCE THOUGHT THAT WHEN THE UNIVERSE WAS DONE EXPANDING, IT WOULD START TO SHRINK. THEY CALL THIS SHRINKING THE "BIG CRUNCH."

It's 380,000 years after the big bang, and the temperature is almost 5,000°F (3,000°C). Clumps of gas form.

One billion years after the big bang, the temperature is -450°F (-255°C). The first galaxies begin to form.

Three billion years after the big bang, the temperature of space reaches what it is today, about -454°F (-270°C).

About nine billion years after the big bang, the sun forms inside the Milky Way galaxy. Earth forms from leftover material at about the same time.

BIODIVERSITY

What do you get when you combine the words *biological* and *diversity?*
Biodiversity! The word was first coined in 1985, and since then,
biodiversity has become a hot topic. Biodiversity means the variety of
forms of life. Think about how many kinds of living things there
are on Earth. They are all connected—through food chains,
carbon cycles, and ties we haven't discovered yet. Each
ecosystem, all living and nonliving things in an area,
depends on its members to maintain balance.
When a species becomes extinct, that balance
is lost. Biodiversity refers to three kinds of
diversity in living things. First, there is
diversity in the types of ecosystems
around the world, such as coral
reefs and savannas. Second,
there is a variety of species
in an area, such as the coral
and plants living with the
glassfish on this reef.
Third, there is variation
within species. The
glassfish shown
here all look like
bubbles, but some
individuals are
faster or longer
than others.
Protecting all
three types of
biodiversity
is the key to
keeping Earth
alive.

PICK AN ECOSYSTEM ►

Hot, cold, wet, dry—you name it! There are all kinds of places where plants and animals live. Each place has a range of temperatures and a range of precipitation that is just the right combination to support the living things in that ecosystem. Take a look at these four ecosystems in West Africa.

Desert: Very few plants and animals can survive the hot, dry Sahara Desert.

Arid Grasslands: The land that borders the desert—called *sahel*, which means "shore"—is home to a few trees, low growing grasses, camels, oxen, and cattle.

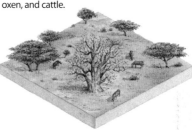

Savanna: A bit more rain here means the savanna ecosystem has more trees and grasses along with the animals, such as giraffes, that eat them.

BIODIVERSITY WITHIN SPECIES ▲

This lioness stalking through the savanna is different in size, strength, and temperament, from other lions of her species. Within each species, there is diversity. This variation in traits is important because passing on helpful traits to offspring will help each species prosper.

Tropical Forest: Thousands of plants and animals live in the moist tropical forest. It is one of Earth's most complex ecosystems.

did you know?.................................
ABOUT 1.75 MILLION SPECIES OF LIVING THINGS ON EARTH HAVE BEEN DESCRIBED AND NAMED, AND MILLIONS MORE ARE WAITING.

The sea anemone provides protection for the clownfish. The clownfish eats parasites off the sea anemone and helps circulate water around the anemone.

◄ BIODIVERSITY BETWEEN SPECIES

Coral reefs teem with millions of species of sponges, coral, algae, and fish. It is the most diverse kind of marine ecosystem, and each species in the coral reef ecosystem interacts with the others. The health of an ecosystem is often measured through its biodiversity. The existence of many species in an ecosystem, with good variation within each species, probably means that each species has plenty of food and shelter.

This clownfish can live among the stinging tentacles of the sea anemone. It is covered with a slimy mucus that protects it from the anemone's poison.

BIOFUELS

Fields of flax, sunflowers, and corn—do they make you think of cars? These plants all play a part in making liquid fuels, called *biofuels*, that can power cars, tractors, buses, and more. Biofuels are made from biomass, which is matter from living things, especially plants. One advantage of using more biofuel is that we use less fossil fuel, such as gasoline. Another benefit is that not only are plants renewable, but the carbon dioxide (CO_2) they release when they burn is balanced by the CO_2 they take in when they grow. Some negatives are that gases are given off during the production and transport of biofuels. The process of clearing land in order to turn it into cropland also generates greenhouse gases. Scientists are hoping that on balance the total output of CO_2 is less, but this is still being debated.

CORN IN YOUR GAS TANK? ▶

One biofuel is ethanol, an alcohol often made from high-starch grains such as corn. Ethanol can be used on its own as a fuel or blended with gasoline. Henry Ford designed the Model T to run on ethanol. Scientists are working on ways to make ethanol from parts of plants that are not food, such as husks, stems, and leaves.

The use of corn is controversial— should the land be used for food or fuel?

did you know?............................
THE DIESEL ENGINE DEMONSTRATED AT THE 1900 WORLD'S FAIR RAN ON PEANUT OIL.

PLANT POWER ▶

These lavender flax and yellow canola plants yield oil that may soon help make biodiesel, another biofuel. Biodiesel is made by mixing alcohol with vegetable oils. Even recycled cooking grease or animal fat can be used. Biodiesel can be added to gasoline or used on its own in diesel engines.

MORE THAN JUST A PRETTY FACE ▲

Though it can be a bit costly, sunflower oil is being looked at as a source for both ethanol and biodiesel fuel. Some farmers make biodiesel fuel from oil extracted from the sunflowers they grow. They mix the oil with lye and alcohol to create biodiesel to fuel their trucks and tractors.

NOT JUST A FAST CAR ▼

This British car, the Vauxhall Astra, runs on 100 percent ethanol. In fact, many racing cars use ethanol because it combusts, or burns, more completely in the engine, giving great performance and reducing emissions and smog. In 2007, the Indy Racing League®, home of the Indianapolis 500®, began using 100 percent ethanol as its official race fuel.

Yellow canola plants   Flax

BIOMIMETICS

A gecko runs across the ceiling. Tiny hairs on its feet help it stick tight without falling. Robots cling to the inside of a volcano, climbing and peeling their feet just like geckos. Are these similarities a coincidence? Not at all. Nature has fantastic designs, and engineers often copy them to make their own inventions better. The mimicry of ideas from nature is called *biomimetics*. Many Olympic swimmers wear suits with bumps like those on a shark to help them move quickly through the water. A swarm of ants seems to wander in all directions, yet there aren't many collisions, so traffic engineers have tracked the ups, downs, ins, and outs of an ant colony to improve the flow of car and airplane traffic. Organisms have had many generations to develop great designs and adaptations—and people are realizing that we can learn from them.

did you know? ONE COMPANY IMPROVED THE FUEL EFFICIENCY OF A CAR BY MODELING ITS DESIGN ON THE SHAPE OF A FISH.

HITCHING A RIDE ▼

In 1948, Swiss engineer George de Mestral walked through the woods with his dog. Afterward, he pulled hundreds of burs from his pants and from his dog's fur. These sticky burs contained the seeds for the burdock plant. On each bur, he noticed a star of spines with a tiny hook at the end. The hooks grabbed onto a passing animal and the seeds inside hitched a ride to spread the plant through the woods and fields.

The nylon hooks on one side of a fastener grab loops of fabric on the other side and cling tightly until they are straightened by an upward force. _____

The hooks on the bur from the burdock plant helped it spread its seeds worldwide.

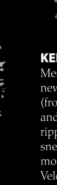

KEEPING THINGS TOGETHER ▶

Mestral used his observations to create a new fastener, which he named Velcro® (from the French words for "velvet" and "hook"). You know the familiar ripping sound of this fastener on your sneakers, jacket, and backpack, but it has more exotic uses, too. Astronauts use Velcro in their helmets and to keep tools in place in zero gravity. Velcro even held a human heart together during the first artificial heart surgery.

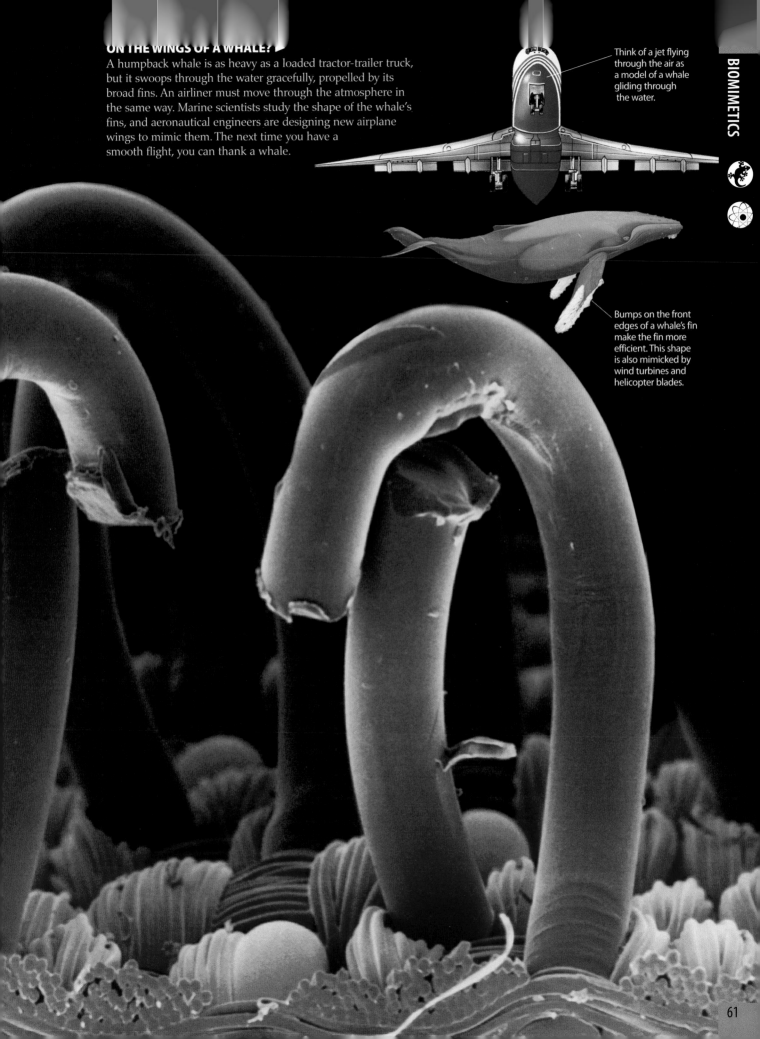

ON THE WINGS OF A WHALE?

A humpback whale is as heavy as a loaded tractor-trailer truck, but it swoops through the water gracefully, propelled by its broad fins. An airliner must move through the atmosphere in the same way. Marine scientists study the shape of the whale's fins, and aeronautical engineers are designing new airplane wings to mimic them. The next time you have a smooth flight, you can thank a whale.

Think of a jet flying through the air as a model of a whale gliding through the water.

Bumps on the front edges of a whale's fin make the fin more efficient. This shape is also mimicked by wind turbines and helicopter blades.

BIRDS

This diverse and colorful crowd has about 9,000 species of all shapes and sizes. The 2.5-inch (about 6.4-cm) bee hummingbird weighs the same as a dime. The wandering albatross wins for longest wingspan: 11 feet (about 3.4 m). Ostriches can grow to 9 feet (2.7 m) tall. And because most birds can fly, they live almost everywhere, from deserts to the poles. Some species of birds do not travel far in their lifetime, while others migrate huge distances. Setting a nonstop flight record, a female bar-tailed godwit flew 7,257 miles (11,679 km) from Alaska to New Zealand.

Hummingbird

Zebrafinch

Blue tit

Tawny eagle

Emu

King penguin

Pekin duck

Peahen

TOO BIG TO FLY! ▶
Emus have long powerful legs, but very small wings. They cannot fly, but they do run fast—up to 31 miles (almost 50 km) per hour. Other flightless birds include the ostrich, rhea, cassowary, and kiwi.

FANCY FEATHERS ▼

The Indian peacock displays his amazing long tail feathers, called his *train*, to attract a mate. The peacock lifts his train to form a fan. Each feather has eye-like spots of brilliant blue, green, and orange. Some studies show that the more eye spots the peacock has, the more peahens he attracts.

Parakeet

Owl

Swift

TONGUE TWISTER ▶

A green woodpecker has a powerful beak. It also has a long, sensitive tongue that is stored curled up inside its skull. The tip of the tongue is armed with barbs, which keep the ants and grubs the bird eats from wriggling away.

Green woodpecker

Toucan

Flamingo

Pelican

Peacock

did you know?..............................
BECAUSE THEY DON'T HAVE TEETH, BIRDS NEED A SECOND STOMACH, CALLED A *GIZZARD*, TO GRIND UP FOOD.

BIRDS CONTINUED

Birds use food and oxygen for "fuel," and both their frame and "engine" are built for fuel-efficiency. They have lightweight bones, many of which are hollow. For added strength, the bones have honeycombed supports inside. Birds digest food fast, and their large, fast-beating heart pumps nutrients quickly through their body. Their respiratory system is very efficient. Connected to their lungs are air sacs that tuck into spaces throughout the body. These sacs act like pumps, sucking in air and pushing it out of the body, keeping a continuous flow of fresh air to the lungs. The lungs themselves don't contract much. Even so, birds breathe rapidly during flight. Pigeons breathe more than 400 times per minute!

HUNTERS OF THE SKIES ▼

Falcons are streamlined, fast-flying birds of prey, called *raptors,* with long, narrow, pointed wings and long, narrow tails. They feed mainly on other birds and insects, and usually capture their prey in midair. Other raptors include owls, hawks, eagles, and vultures. Most of these birds have excellent eyesight and sharp, hooked bills for tearing at flesh. They are highly skilled fliers.

Most feathers are called *contour* feathers, including the wing and tail feathers, and are aerodynamic devices.

Fuzzy feathers, such as down, are for insulation. Colorful feathers are to attract mates.

Peacock down feather

◄ FEATHERS FOR ALL OCCASIONS

Birds are the only animals that have feathers. There are many types—to insulate, streamline, and waterproof the bird, and to enable flight. Each bird has between 1,000 and 25,000 feathers, depending upon the species and size. The tundra swan has the most on record. Feathers are composed mostly of keratin, the same substance that horns, hooves, and fingernails are made from. Birds molt once or twice each year to replace old, broken, or worn-out feathers with new ones.

Pheasant feathers

Peacock feather

The great hornbill, about 4 feet (about 1.2 m) tall, has a horny growth, called a casque, on top of its bill.

SHAPED FOR EATING ▲

Each type of bird has a bill or beak adapted for its particular diet. The great hornbill's sturdy beak can handle not only its favorite fruit, figs, but small animals. A strong cone-shaped bill helps finches and grosbeaks pick up and crack seeds. Insect-eaters such as warblers have thin, slender, pointed beaks. Hummingbirds have long, strawlike bills to sip nectar from flowers. A merganser grabs fish with the hooked point of its bill and holds it with the bill's jagged edges.

Some raptors can see a rabbit a mile (1.6 km) away.

In flight, the wing feathers closer to the body provide lift. The longer outermost feathers at the tip of the wing pull the bird forward.

Curved, sharp claws, called *talons,* help raptors catch and grip prey.

Tail feathers function as direction-changers and as brakes.

BLACK HOLES

Start with a star 10 times more massive than the sun. When the star dies, its center, or core, collapses, and its outer layers fly out in a spectacular explosion called a *supernova*. The core continues to shrink, becoming a black hole that might be only 20 miles (about 32 km) wide and incredibly dense. Once anything, including a light wave, enters a black hole, it can never leave. All of the mass of a black hole is at its center in a point called a *singularity*. In a sense, the singularity is a hole in the universe that soaks up matter and energy.

Matter spiraling around the black hole is called its *accretion disk*. Until it gets very close, this matter does not act any differently than matter around a large star.

As the matter gets very close to the black hole, it gains energy and heats to several million degrees.

STAR POWER ▼

Gravity pulls a star's mass toward its core. This inward pressure balances the outward pressure from the energy that is created when stars combine lighter elements, such as helium and carbon, into heavier ones, such as oxygen. This process of combining elements is called *fusion*. Big stars can produce enough heat to continue fusing elements—until they get to iron. Fusing iron with other elements uses energy rather than creating it, so fusion stops. Then gravity wins, and the star collapses.

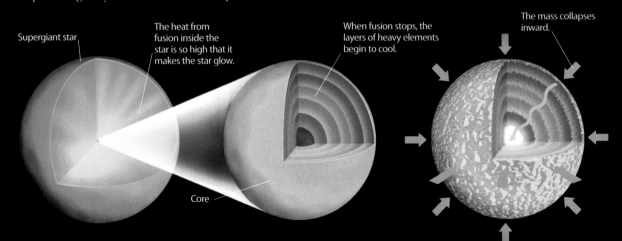

Supergiant star

The heat from fusion inside the star is so high that it makes the star glow.

When fusion stops, the layers of heavy elements begin to cool.

The mass collapses inward.

Core

The matter moves faster and faster, picking up energy. High-energy matter sends out high-energy radiation. Back home in the solar system, we use space telescopes to grab photos of the X-rays that come from really, really hot, high-energy matter.

Some of the matter around the rapidly spinning black hole flies off at speeds near the speed of light. The X-ray energy emitted by these jets of matter is evidence of the black hole.

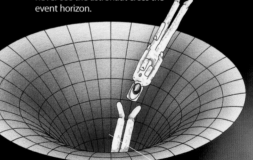

If you could watch as the astronaut moved toward the hole, she would appear to move more and more slowly. You would never see the astronaut cross the event horizon.

The boundary beyond which light cannot escape is called the *event horizon*. This is the black hole's diameter as viewed from the outside.

At the event horizon, the light takes almost forever to get away from the black hole, so an image of the astronaut remains long after the astronaut has passed.

DOWN THE HOLE ▶

What would you see if you watched someone fall into a black hole? The term "spaghettification" was coined after physicist Stephen Hawking said the astronaut in the illustration resembled a piece of spaghetti being pulled long and thin. The fantastic mass of the black hole exerts a great gravitational force on objects when they are very close. The force is much stronger on the astronaut's head than on her feet, causing her body to stretch longer and longer.

No one knows what happens beyond the event horizon because no information ever comes back out to us.

OOD PRESSURE

're lifting something heavy or about to take a big test, you might feel "under ure." This pressure isn't all in your head. Your blood vessels are under real ure. Blood pressure is the force of blood pushing against the inner walls of blood s. When your heart squeezes during a heartbeat, blood is pushed into the blood s, increasing the pressure inside. This higher pressure during heartbeats is called *ic pressure*. When your heart rests between beats, the lower pressure is called *olic pressure*. Doctors use the two pressure readings to describe blood pressure. night have heard your doctor or an actor on TV say, "Her blood pressure is 112 72." Normal adult blood pressure measures 119/79 or lower, in which 119 is ystolic pressure and 79 is the diastolic pressure. Pressure of 120/80 or above is dered high. Having blood pressure of 140/90 or higher most of the time is called *tension*, which can increase risk of heart failure, stroke, or kidney failure. Having pressure of 120–139 systolic over 80–89 diastolic is called *prehypertension*, n can lead to hypertension.

Artery

White blood cell

Red blood cell

Lining

Inner layer
Elastic fibers
Muscle layer
Elastic fibers

Outer layer

HEALTHY ARTERIES ▶
Arteries are blood vessels that carry blood away from the heart. They are made of layers of elastic fibers and muscle tissue. Blood pressure tends to increase as people reach their 40s and 50s, and in some families more than others. There are many causes, and the condition can develop without showing any symptoms. People can lower their risk of developing high blood pressure by eating healthy foods, exercising, and not smoking.

Lifting heavy weights in one quick movement dramatically increases blood pressure. Tests of athletes have recorded temporary increases in blood pressure to 320/250.

MEASURING BLOOD PRESSURE ▶

Doctors use stethoscopes and a tool called a *sphygmomanometer* to measure blood pressure. The tool has a pressure cuff that goes around your arm. A hand pump fills the cuff with air. The pressure increases, cutting off blood flow in your arm. The doctor slowly releases the cuff's pressure and listens for the sound of your blood flowing with the stethoscope. The reading when the blood flow returns is the systolic pressure. The reading when the blood flow can no longer be heard, indicating your heart is between beats, is the diastolic pressure.

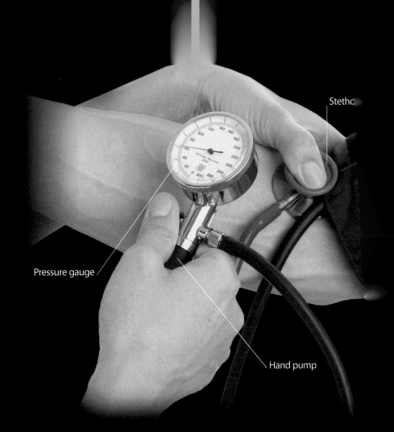

Stetho

Pressure gauge

Hand pump

◀ CHANGES IN BLOOD PRESSURE

Your blood pressure is usually lower when you are sleeping or relaxed, and it rises when you are under physical and mental stress. Exercise increases your blood pressure temporarily, as the heart beats faster and pushes blood through the blood vessels at a greater rate. People who exercise regularly experience a smaller increase in heart rate with physical activity, and tend to have lower blood pressure overall.

did you
know?...................
POLICE MAY MEASURE BLOOD PRESSURE AS PART OF A LIE DETECTOR TEST, BECAUSE PRESSURE OFTEN GOES UP WHEN SOMEONE IS LYING.

BLOOD TYPES

Bags of blood? These bags may seem like props for a horror movie, but they actually save lives. Every two and a half seconds, someone in the world donates a pint (0.5 L) of blood. During donation, a nurse sticks a needle into a vein in the donor's arm, sending blood through a tube and into a bag. The blood is tested, and if it is free of disease, it becomes part of a blood bank. It may save a premature baby or a car crash victim. If someone needs blood, a bag of blood is connected through a tube into a patient's vein. The donor blood flows into the patient; this is called a *transfusion*. The donor and patient are strangers, but they have one thing in common: their blood type.

Donation: Blood donation is safe. The average adult body contains about 10 pints (5 L) of blood. A healthy donor's body will replace the blood cells lost from a donation within weeks.

Donation: People can receive transfusions only of human blood.

Parts: Blood banks separate donor whole blood into its parts: red blood cells, white blood cells, plasma, and platelets. Patients usually need only a single blood component instead of whole blood.

Parts: About 45% of whole blood is made up of red blood cells, which carry oxygen. If you do not have enough healthy red blood cells, you may feel tired due to a lack of oxygen.

Parts: Less than 1% of blood is made up of white blood cells, which attack germs. White blood cells float in plasma and can race to wherever they are needed.

Parts: About 55% of blood is plasma, a yellow liquid containing mostly water. Dissolved in the plasma are vitamins, hormones, and some minerals.

did you know?..............................
A RED BLOOD CELL TRAVELS OVER 300 MILES (480 KM) THROUGH BLOOD VESSELS BEFORE IT DIES.

Antigens: Antigens are chemical molecules that sit on the surface of red blood cells. Two antigens, A and B, are the basis for the commonly used ABO system of blood typing.

Antigens: Type A blood has A antigens on its red blood cells; type B blood has B antigens; type AB blood has both; and type O blood has neither.

Antigens: The antigens in blood will make antibodies, which attack a different antigen. Type A antibodies will attack type B blood, and type B antibodies will attack type A blood.

Parts: Platelets also float around in your plasma. Platelets are sticky and help clot blood. Without platelets, you could bleed to death.

Types: People have different color eyes and hair. These are traits you can see. People also have many genetic characteristics you cannot see, such as blood type. You can have blood type A, B, AB, or O.

Types: If one of your parents has type A or B and the other has type O, you could be either type A, B, or O.

BODY PROTECTION

The race car clips the wall, spins through the air, lands upside down, and catches on fire. The driver? He wriggles out unharmed, thanks to his helmet, firesuit, and other protective gear. Protective equipment routinely saves firefighters, police officers, and soldiers from serious injury or death. Skateboarders, bike riders, and athletes have helmets, pads, and other protectors to use. Thousands of years ago, helmets and body armor were made from stiff animal skins. As technology advanced, body protection improved to metal plates that have now given way to today's lighter, sturdier synthetics. Bulletproof vests have saved countless lives, but comfort is still a challenge. So new "liquid armor" is being developed. It lets the wearer move freely, but when an object hits, the armor instantly stiffens to stop it. Whatever you like to do, make sure you can keep doing it: wear safety gear.

IRON MAN ▲

Heavy metal? Yes! A suit of battle armor in the Middle Ages weighed between 45 and 55 pounds (about 20 to 25 kg). Iron plate is hard, strong, and difficult to pierce with swords, arrows, and similar weapons. Metal plates could not stop bullets and explosives, so eventually they gave way to other materials.

HOT STUFF ►

Different fires require different suits. Every layer in firefighters' clothing, including the thread that holds the suit together, has to protect them without igniting, melting, or tearing. Most firefighters wear what is called a *structural suit,* for fighting fires in buildings. Fires that burn at very high temperatures, such as airport fires that are burning liquid fuel, require what's called *proximity suits,* such as the ones shown here. Proximity gear has a metallic coating that reflects heat away from the firefighter.

◄ EYES, EARS, ETC.

Protective gear isn't just for knights, firefighters, and other heroes. Planning to build something? Goggles and safety glasses save your eyes from flying objects. Ear protectors muffle the deafening sound of power tools. A helmet can prevent a hospital trip to treat a head injury. Sturdy work gloves reduce blisters, and knee pads protect these fragile joints. Whatever the risk, there is probably safety equipment to help prevent it.

Helmet with face guard

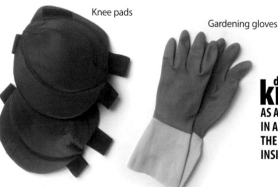

Knee pads

Gardening gloves

Hearing protection

Ear plugs

did you know?..............
AS A BICYCLE HELMET CRUSHES IN A CRASH, IT SLOWS DOWN THE LANDING FOR THE HEAD INSIDE IT.

A thin, transparent coating of gold on the face shield protects the face from heat.

Suits treated with aluminum reflect intense heat radiating from a large fire, allowing firefighters to approach the flames.

How the layers of a fire suit protect the wearer from the outside to the inside

Antistatic layer to keep static from starting a fire

Liquid chemicals stopped by top layers

Tough flexible outer shell

Moisture barrier

Strong flame-resistant layer

Soft liquid-resistant layer

Body heat released through layers

73

BPA

Is plastic bad for you? Let's look at the evidence. Scientific studies have shown that a chemical called *bisphenol A*, or BPA, that is used to make some plastics harms developing animals. More studies are being conducted to see how BPA affects humans. Some studies suggest that it could affect the development of fetuses, infants, and children. People eat foods and drink liquids that contain BPA at the levels that were tested with animals. The Centers for Disease Control (CDC) found BPA in the urine of 93 percent of 2,517 people tested in 2003. Some refillable plastic water bottles, plastic utensils, baby bottles, and food containers contain BPA. Cans are often lined with BPA-containing coatings to keep the food from touching the can. The chemical can leach into food from these containers. Heat causes BPA to leach more quickly. In 2009, Canada declared BPA a human health hazard. Japan has eliminated most BPA from cans and plastics.

did you know?
GLOBAL PRODUCTION OF BPA IN 2003 WAS ESTIMATED TO BE MORE THAN 2 MILLION TONS. ALMOST HALF OF THAT WAS USED IN THE UNITED STATES!

BPA FREE ▲
Those hard, clear, refillable plastic water bottles that come in many colors used to be made of plastic called *polycarbonate*, which contained BPA. As people become more aware of the possible dangers of BPA, more manufacturers are making bottles that are BPA free or offering stainless steel water bottles.

WHAT'S YOUR NUMBER? ▼

Most of the millions of bottles that are discarded—and in some cases, recycled— do not contain BPA. Plastics that contain BPA are hard. Soft plastics, such as those used in one-use water or soda bottles, do not contain BPA. Plastics with the recycling number 7 may contain BPA.

CANNED BPA ▶

Researchers found BPA in more than half of the canned foods they tested. Chicken soup, infant formula, and ravioli had the highest BPA levels. A person who eats from one to three servings of these foods can ingest BPA at levels that cause serious harm in animals.

There are no limits on the amount of BPA used in canned goods in the United States.

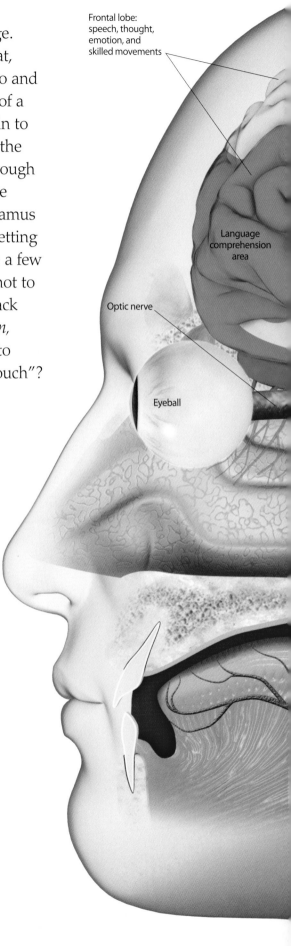

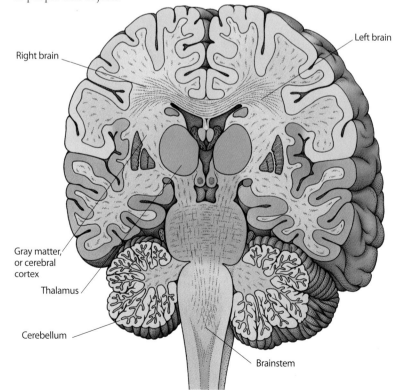

BRAIN POWER

For nearly everything you do, a part of your brain is in charge. The brainstem controls your most basic functions—heartbeat, breathing, digestion. The brainstem also relays messages into and out of other parts of your brain. When you feel the warmth of a campfire, the sensation travels through nerves from your skin to your spinal cord and into your brainstem. You move toward the fire—the command to move went from your cerebellum through your brainstem and out to your muscles. You reach out to the fire—ouch! But by the time the pain signal gets to your thalamus and it tells the gray matter of your brain that your hand is getting too warm, your hand is already pulling away. That's because a few messages are too urgent to wait. As soon as the news "Too hot to handle!" reaches your spinal cord, "Get out, NOW!" starts back toward your hand. Pulling back is what's called a *reflex action*, which travels from your hand to your spinal cord and back to your hand, without going through your brain. And saying "ouch"? Thank the speech area of your brain.

RIGHT IS LEFT, LEFT IS RIGHT ▼

The brain is divided into two halves, called *hemispheres*. Although the two sides of the brain look symmetrical—the same on both sides—they handle different tasks. While you read these words, your left brain works more. Or at least that's the case for almost all right-handed people. About 40 percent of left-handed people use either the right hemisphere or the whole brain for language. The right brain appears to be more involved in visual recognition of people and objects.

Frontal lobe: speech, thought, emotion, and skilled movements

Language comprehension area

Optic nerve

Eyeball

Right brain

Left brain

Gray matter, or cerebral cortex

Thalamus

Cerebellum

Brainstem

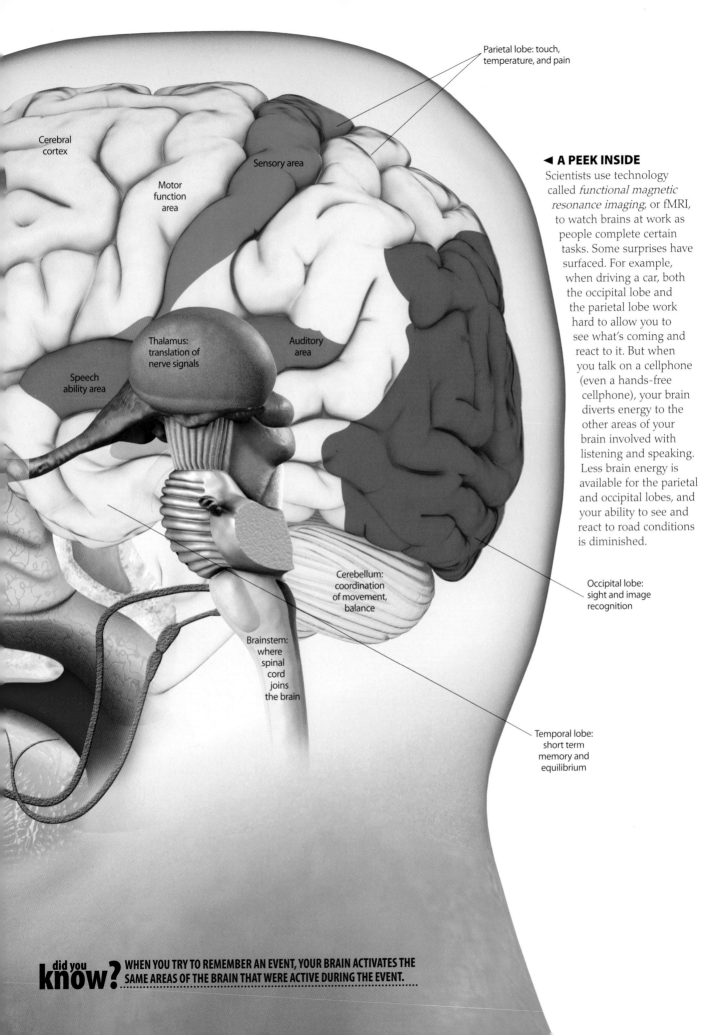

Parietal lobe: touch,
temperature, and pain

Cerebral
cortex

Sensory area

Motor
function
area

Thalamus:
translation of
nerve signals

Auditory
area

Speech
ability area

Cerebellum:
coordination
of movement,
balance

Brainstem:
where
spinal
cord
joins
the brain

◄ A PEEK INSIDE

Scientists use technology
called *functional magnetic
resonance imaging*, or fMRI,
to watch brains at work as
people complete certain
tasks. Some surprises have
surfaced. For example,
when driving a car, both
the occipital lobe and
the parietal lobe work
hard to allow you to
see what's coming and
react to it. But when
you talk on a cellphone
(even a hands-free
cellphone), your brain
diverts energy to the
other areas of your
brain involved with
listening and speaking.
Less brain energy is
available for the parietal
and occipital lobes, and
your ability to see and
react to road conditions
is diminished.

Occipital lobe:
sight and image
recognition

Temporal lobe:
short term
memory and
equilibrium

did you know? WHEN YOU TRY TO REMEMBER AN EVENT, YOUR BRAIN ACTIVATES THE
SAME AREAS OF THE BRAIN THAT WERE ACTIVE DURING THE EVENT.

BRIDGES

To cross over a creek, you find a log that reaches from one bank to the other. The log holds up your weight and keeps your feet out of the water—as long as you can balance! You are demonstrating Newton's third law of motion: for every action, there is an equal and opposite reaction. Your body pushes down on the log. The log and the points on the banks where it rests react by pushing up with equal force. The weight the bridge can hold is called the *load*. The length of the bridge is the *span*. Throughout history, people have found ingenious ways to carry heavier loads over longer spans. Both bridges shown here use one of the oldest forms, an arch, to help support the load across the span.

The two main cables pull like a bow string on the anchorages.

BRIDGES AND HAMMOCKS ▶

Think of a hammock, held up by ropes attached to trees. This suspension bridge is held up by two giant cables—3 feet (about 1 m) in diameter. The cables are draped over towers and attached on each end to a 60,000-ton concrete structure, called an *anchorage*, where the bridge is attached to the ground. Smaller cables suspend the weight from the two main cables. The cables distribute the load over the towers and out to the anchorages.

From end to end, the Golden Gate Bridge stretches 8,981 feet (2,737 m) across San Francisco Bay.

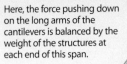

The main towers reach 746 feet (227 m) above the water and about 110 feet (34 m) below the water.

Here, the force pushing down on the long arms of the cantilevers is balanced by the weight of the structures at each end of this span.

CANTILEVERS AT WORK ▲

The Firth of Forth Bridge in Scotland, at 8,276 feet (2,523 m) long, is one of the world's longest cantilever bridges. A cantilever is a type of lever whose long end sticks out over the water, like a huge, very stiff diving board. The short end is held down by enormous weights. Two cantilevers, one coming from each end of a span, can be joined in the middle to form a bridge.

The center span of the bridge, between the towers, is the suspended portion. At 4,200 feet (1,280 m) long, it is now dwarfed by Japan's Akashi-Kaikyo bridge— the longest suspension— at 6,532 feet (1,991 m).

**did you
know?**....................
ON THE GOLDEN GATE BRIDGE, THE MAIN CABLES SIT ON THE TOP OF THE TOWER IN HUGE STEEL SADDLES.

BROKEN BONES

A bone is like a tree branch. You can bend it gently, but too much pressure will snap it in two. A bone break is called a *fracture*. Bones can crack, without breaking all the way across—sometimes called a *hairline fracture*. Under the pressure of a car accident, for example, bones may shatter. Bones can even stick out through the skin. A broken bone and the injured tissue around it hurt a lot. If the two— or more—parts of the broken bone are no longer connected or lined up, a doctor will align the parts, and then immobilize the bone with a splint, cast, or brace. Immobilizing the bone is important because movement can cause damage to the bone, nearby blood vessels, nerves, or tissue around the bone. After a few months, a broken bone can heal so well that even an X-ray can't show where the break was.

did you know?....................
THE MOST COMMON FRACTURE IS JUST ABOVE THE WRIST. PEOPLE INSTINCTIVELY REACH OUT TO BREAK A FALL.

BONE REPAIR ▶

Fractures heal by forming new bone, not scar tissue. A fracture severs blood vessels in the bone. The blood forms a clot between the two pieces of broken bone. After a few days, cartilage cells begin to replace the clot. Cartilage is strong connective tissue that is more flexible than bone. This process continues for about three weeks. Then soft bone cells begin to replace the cartilage cells. This rebuilding process lasts for three to four months. Over several more months, hard bone cells replace the soft bone cells.

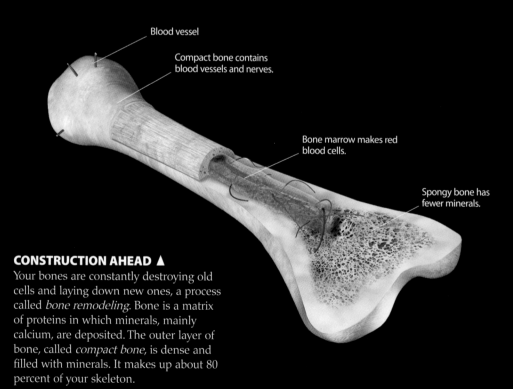

Blood vessel

Compact bone contains blood vessels and nerves.

Bone marrow makes red blood cells.

Spongy bone has fewer minerals.

CONSTRUCTION AHEAD ▲

Your bones are constantly destroying old cells and laying down new ones, a process called *bone remodeling*. Bone is a matrix of proteins in which minerals, mainly calcium, are deposited. The outer layer of bone, called *compact bone*, is dense and filled with minerals. It makes up about 80 percent of your skeleton.

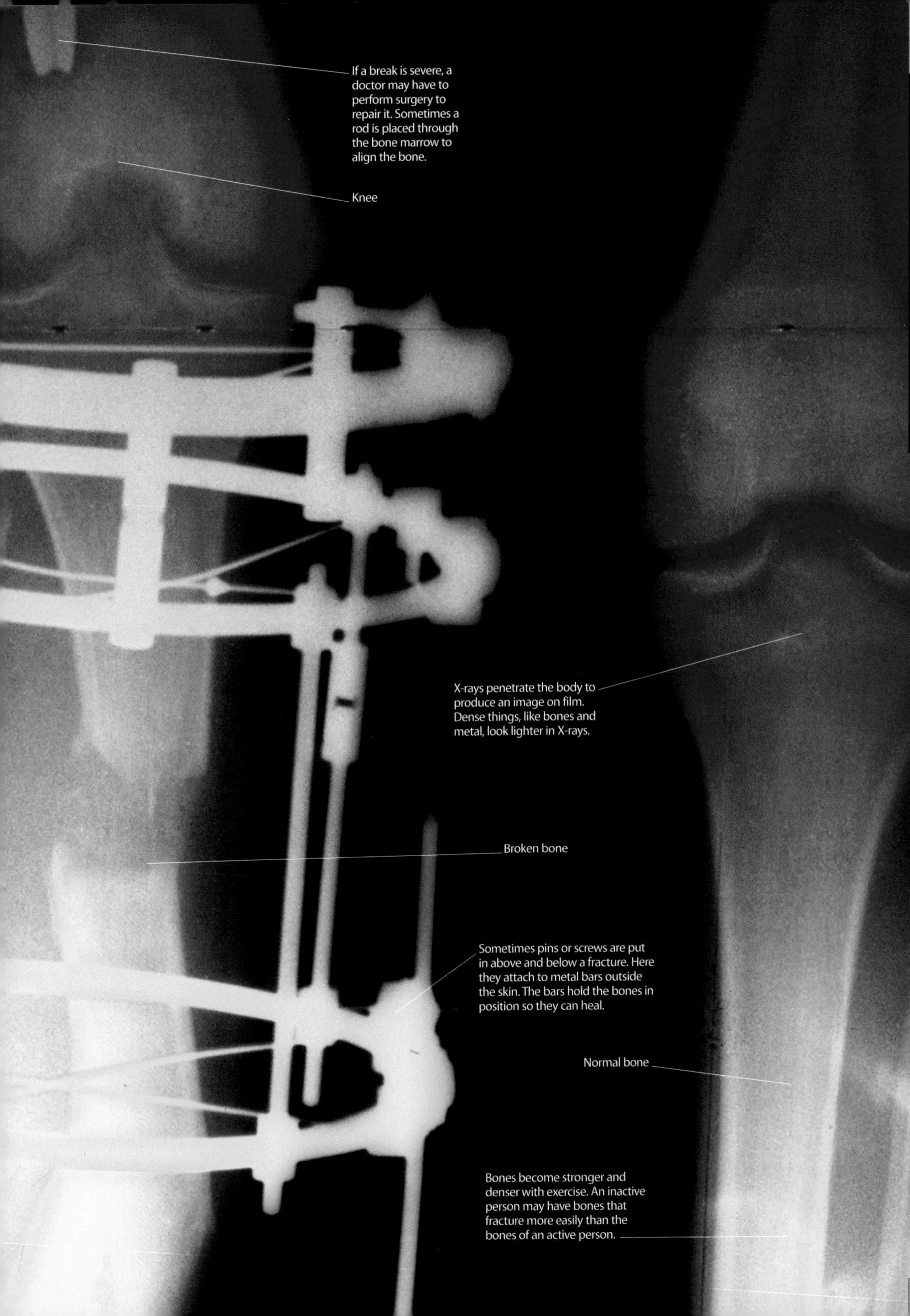

If a break is severe, a doctor may have to perform surgery to repair it. Sometimes a rod is placed through the bone marrow to align the bone.

Knee

X-rays penetrate the body to produce an image on film. Dense things, like bones and metal, look lighter in X-rays.

Broken bone

Sometimes pins or screws are put in above and below a fracture. Here they attach to metal bars outside the skin. The bars hold the bones in position so they can heal.

Normal bone

Bones become stronger and denser with exercise. An inactive person may have bones that fracture more easily than the bones of an active person.

BUNGEE JUMPING

Cowabunga! In search of a thrill, bungee jumpers leap from bridges, mountain ledges, buildings, cranes, and even helicopters. The higher the starting point, the more gravitational potential energy the jumper stores. When the jumper steps into the air, that stored energy is transformed into kinetic energy and then to elastic potential energy in the bungee cord. This energy transformation flip flops as the jumper rebounds multiple times before coming to a rest. With a good all-rubber cord, a person can rebound with 85 percent of the energy of the original jump. Some energy is transformed into thermal energy. There is not enough data to assess the safety of the sport. Matching the equipment to the weight of the jumper is crucial. The cords used today are an improvement over those used by the earliest jumpers. Pacific islanders proved their courage by tying vines to their ankles and jumping from trees or towers.

❶ JUMPING
The weight of the jumper determines how elastic a cord the jumper will use.

❷ FALLING
A harness, plus another for backup, is attached to a jumper's ankles, body, or chest and shoulders.

3 REBOUNDING
Jumpers typically
rebound 2 to 4 times.

BUNGEE'S ELASTIC MAGIC ▲

As the bungee cord stretches, the kinetic energy is transformed
into stored energy in the cord's rubber strands. The more the
cord stretches, the more elastic potential energy it stores. Before
hitting bottom, all of a person's kinetic energy is robbed by the
bungee cord and the person stops falling and bounces back up.
With each bounce some of the energy is transferred to heat. The
bouncing stops when all of the person's original gravitational
potential energy is transformed into thermal energy.

did you
know?..
SOME BUNGEE CORDS CAN STRETCH UP TO 4 TIMES
THEIR RESTING LENGTH DURING A JUMP!

BUOYS

On land, it's easy to put up a direction sign—just attach it to a post in the ground. How about a cellphone transmitter? No problem. Build a tower and bolt the transmitter at the top. In the ocean, though, you can't just hang things on a post or tower. That's where buoys come in. A buoy is basically a hollow float that is moored, or anchored, to the floor of the ocean or bay. Once the buoy is in place, you have something that can hold a sign, a light, or a complex, computerized communication system. Buoys can be used for navigation aids, scientific monitoring, and tsunami detection. Some buoys include an entire weather station, constantly beaming data to a distant satellite, which relays information in turn to a meteorologist on land. Data from systems on these buoys are combined and analyzed so that weather forecasts can be radioed to ships at sea.

WHICH WAY DO I GO? ▼

As a boat navigates a channel, the captain needs to know where the water is deep enough for safe passage. Navigation buoys are the traffic signs of the water. In the Americas, red buoys mark the right side, called *starboard*, of a channel for a ship returning to harbor; green buoys mark the left side, called *port*. Combinations of colors, as well as the shapes at the top of the buoy, called *topmarks*, can indicate safe water, restricted areas, and the compass direction, called the *cardinal*, of the safe side to pass.

A port channel cone mark

A safe water sphere mark

◄ WAVE WATCHERS

A network of tsunami detection stations is anchored on the sea floor, this one in Indonesia. A detector on the sea bottom reads the temperature and pressure of the surrounding water and records that information. A radio transmitter on the buoy sends the information to a satellite, which relays it to a computer at the control center. Data from this system of buoys help scientists detect tsunamis as they develop. Warnings are given to people along coastal areas.

did you know?
....
SOME NAVIGATION BUOYS WEIGH UP TO 10 TONS. THEY ARE ATTACHED TO HUGE CONCRETE BLOCKS BENEATH THE WATER TO KEEP THEM UPRIGHT AND IN PLACE.

Topmark for safe water

Topmark for danger

Ladder

An antirotating fin keeps the
buoy from spinning.

A safe water
pillar mark means
safe water on
any side.

Topmark for north

Lantern

Solar panel

An isolated danger
pillar mark is moored
on or near danger.

A north cardinal
pillar mark indicates
that the safest
passage is on the
north side.

Warning lantern

This radar
transmitter
sends out a
signal that
allows ships
to find the
buoy, even on
a foggy night.

MARKING THE CHANNEL ▶

Even a simple channel marker can be a
fairly complicated buoy. This port mark
includes a warning lantern on top, with the
color of the light matching the color of the
buoy for night or rough weather navigation.
Power must be available for these devices
so the buoy must have a large battery. Some
buoys use solar power to keep the battery
charged.

Looking a little like a lemur and a bit like a bat, bush babies are peculiar primates. The little mammals live in African forests and bush land. Bush babies got their name from British explorers who thought the small, tree-dwelling animals sounded like crying babies. Like their cousins the lemurs, bush babies are nocturnal—they sleep in tree hollows during the day and hunt and forage at night. Unlike you and me, bush babies are pros at moving around in the dark. They use long hind limbs to leap from tree to tree, hunting insects, socializing, and marking their territory. Some bush babies can leap more than 20 feet (6 m)! Bush babies are wooly and grey to brown in color. They range in size from 6 to 9 inches (15–23 cm) long, not including their bushy tail, which is another 9 inches (23 cm) long.

did you know?..................
BUSH BABIES WIPE URINE ONTO THEIR HANDS AND FEET TO HELP THEM MARK TERRITORY AS THEY JUMP THROUGH THE TREES.

Each eye is equipped with a highly reflective layer, called the *tapetum*, that helps capture light for excellent night vision.

Bush babies have a moist, leathery nose and a great sense of smell.

Bush babies' fingers and toes end in flat, fleshy pads that give them an excellent grip.

◄ SUPER SENSES

It's a bird! It's a plane! It's a…bush baby! These little primates have superhero senses that allow them to move around at night. Their large, sensitive eyes have pupils that expand at night to let in light. Ridged, bat-like ears move independently to help locate quiet insect prey. A long bushy tail acts as a rudder to help steer the bush baby as it "flies" between branches.

BUTTERFLIES

Yellow and red, orange and blue—butterflies come in all colors, not to mention shapes and sizes. But how and why are butterflies so colorful? Butterfly and moth wings are covered in tiny overlapping rows of scales, like shingles covering a house. Each scale is made up of even tinier structures, called *nanostructures*. These crystal-like shapes scatter light in a way that produces single colors and rainbowlike shimmering, called *iridescence*. Some scales also contain colorful chemicals, called *pigments*. Coloration helps attract mates, warn off predators, and camouflage the insect as it feeds on flower nectar.

Mapwing, common in Malaysia

Ruddy daggerwing, from the southern United States

Most butterflies have club-shaped antennae.

Australian imperial white's colorful underside

Owl butterfly

One of the many blue morphos of South America

Compound eye, with hundreds of lenses

◄ **COOL PARTS**
Butterflies see color very well, an adaptation that helps them find each other and spot flowers. Most of the butterflies shown here are from the brush-footed family. Their short front legs end in brushes used for sensing. They walk on their back four legs.

Butterflies sip nectar by uncurling their proboscis, a mouth part that is like a straw.

Male danaid eggfly, from India

Brush-footed butterfly from Paraguay

did you
know?
THE WORLD'S LARGEST BUTTERFLY—THE QUEEN ALEXANDRA'S BIRDWING—IS FOUND IN NEW GUINEA AND HAS A 12-INCH (30 CM) WINGSPAN.

The small hairstreak butterfly from Southeast Asia

Female danaid eggflies mimic an African butterfly that tastes bad.

Malay lacewing

HAZARDOUS HUES ▶
African giant swallowtails are brightly colored butterflies that count on being recognized by predators. They are poisonous, so predators learn to avoid them. Some perfectly edible butterflies have coloring that mimics that of a bad-tasting or poisonous butterfly, so predators avoid them, too.

Wingspan of about 10 inches (25 cm)

The eye spots of the banana eater from New Guinea trick predators by looking like the eyes of a much larger animal.

This Bolivian butterfly could pass for a fungus-covered dead leaf.

CACTUS

Anyone who thinks that plants are harmless has probably never met a cactus. One accidental kick with a sandaled foot and you'll be pulling painful spines out of your tender toes. When you picture a cactus, you probably think of its thick shape, waxy outer covering, and, of course, those prickly, sharp spines. All of these features help the cactus survive in the dry, open deserts, mostly in North and South America. Cactuses, like all other plants, are made up of cells. Rigid cell walls give cells their shape and protect them. Plant cells contain chloroplasts, which look something like green jelly beans, to help the plant make food using the sun's energy. All plants, including cactuses, require carbon dioxide and water, along with the sun's energy, to make their food.

Cactuses grow new flesh only from the top of the plant and the tips of the branches.

LEAVES OR STEMS? ▼

These broad, flat parts of the prickly pear cactus may look like leaves, but they are actually the stems of the plant. Cactuses do have leaves, though. Many cactus leaves are microscopic. Some cactuses grow very small, pointy leaves, which eventually fall off. Small or absent leaves reduce the surface area through which the plant could lose moisture.

Sharp spines protect the cactus from being eaten. Tufts of hair may shade the plant.

did you know? THE TALLEST CACTUS IN THE WORLD IS MORE THAN 60 FEET (18 M).

◄ **THICK BODIES**

The thick shape of a cactus helps it store water. It also reduces the amount of surface area that is exposed to the hot sun and dry air. This means that the cactus loses less water to evaporation. This saguaro cactus is supported by woody ribs inside. The pleats of flesh over the ribs expand like an accordion to store water after a rain.

A saguaro can live more than 150 years, but it may not develop branches until it is 50 years old.

CACTUS CONTINUED

Cactuses produce flowers that are not only colorful, but useful, too. Often, the flowers bloom at night. They are pollinated by insects that are active in the cooler night air. Once pollinated, many cactus flowers form sweet, juicy, brightly colored fruit. Fruit attracts animals, who spread the seeds when they carry the fruit away from the plant or leave undigested seeds in their droppings. These seeds can produce new cactuses, but not until the conditions are right. The seeds may stay dormant for long periods of time. Only when there is enough water will seeds start to grow and form new plants. Many cactuses also reproduce when a piece of the stem is broken off. New roots form where that part of the stem touches the ground. Then a new plant can grow.

JUICY FRUITS ▼

Some cactus fruits are sold in markets as a tasty snack. The pitahaya, or yellow dragon fruit, tastes like a melon.

A pitahaya has white juicy flesh with crunchy black seeds.

Area of new growth

Thick cactus stem

Long root to find moisture

◄ THIRSTY ROOTS

Some cactuses have widespread, thin roots that absorb water and give them support in dry, sandy soil. Others grow thick roots that let them store water underground, away from the drying sun.

UNUSUAL FLOWERS ►

Some cactuses look very different when they grow old enough to reproduce. Some Melocactus species, for example, grow a bristly red turban on top of their green bodies. Flowers grow from this mature part of the cactus, and the flowers form seeds.

Young part of cactus

Mature part of cactus

Defensive, needle-
like spines _____

**PROTECTIVE
PRICKLES ▶**
Even the fruit of
the many species
of prickly pear
cactus are often
covered with barbed
spines, called
glochids. Fruit can be
green, red, or purple.
The cactus's sharp
spines discourage
thirsty animals from
eating its moist flesh.
Surrounding the spines
are tufts of hair that
can be a challenge to
remove when people pick and
use the fruit. People eat prickly
pear cactus fruits raw or make
them into jelly and candy.

**did you
know?**..................................
CHEFS REMOVE THE NEEDLES FROM PRICKLY PEAR
CACTUS PADS, SLICE THE PADS, AND COOK THEM TO
MAKE A POPULAR MEXICAN DISH CALLED *NOPALITOS*.

CAMOUFLAGE

For people who are not hunters or soldiers, wearing camouflage may be a fashion statement. For animals, on the other hand, having camouflage can be a matter of life or death. Camouflage is body coloration and texture that helps an animal blend in with its surroundings. Predators—animals that hunt and kill their food—and prey—those who are hunted—both make good use of camouflage. A tiger has dark vertical stripes on its orange coat. This coloring makes the tiger difficult to see as the tiger hides in tall grasses and sneaks up on its prey. A walking stick is an insect that has a body the color, texture, and shape of a stick. The insect blends in among real sticks when predators are nearby.

NOW YOU DON'T SEE ME ▼

The thorny devil lizard is a small reptile, about 4–6 inches (10–15 cm) in length, that lives in Australia. It can change color rapidly. It has a pointy hump on the back of its neck that might look like an extra head. When a predator is near, the lizard may tuck its real head between its legs, presumably so the predator will go for the fake head.

The pointed thorns on the lizard's back offer protection and also help it blend in with the textures of its surroundings.

The camouflage pattern of colors looks like the surrounding pebbles.

WHAT FISH? ▶

The American plaice is a type of flatfish that, as an adult, swims on its side. Its left eye actually moves over to its right side as it develops! Having two eyes on one side allows the fish to see clearly when it lies flat on the sandy bottom of the Atlantic Ocean, where it lives. Because the upper side of the fish is brown and speckled, it blends in well with its surroundings.

The head, when seen from above, matches the coloring of the bare twig.

CHAMELEON COLOR ▲

The Parson's chameleon lives in the forests of Madagascar. It is one of the largest chameleons, up to 24 inches (61 cm) long, with a tongue even longer than that. A chameleon cannot purposefully change its skin color to match its surroundings. Its color changes in response to mood, fear, and temperature.

The color and texture of the legs match the lichen on the twig.

did you know?.....................
IT TAKES MORE THAN A YEAR AND A HALF FOR A BABY PARSON'S CHAMELEON TO HATCH FROM ITS EGG. THEN IT IS FULLY DEVELOPED AND ON ITS OWN.

CANCER TREATMENT

You may know of someone who died from cancer, but you may also know of someone whose cancer was cured. Cancer is a group of diseases in which abnormal cells grow and divide in an uncontrolled way. These cells can invade surrounding tissue or spread to other parts of the body. The form of cancer treatment depends on the type of cancer and whether it has spread. Some abnormal growths, or tumors, can be completely removed by surgery. If the cancer has spread, however, doctors may treat it with drugs, a process called *chemotherapy* or *chemo*. They may also treat the cancer with radiation, called *radiation therapy* or *radiotherapy*. Sometimes doctors use both treatments together to destroy cancer cells.

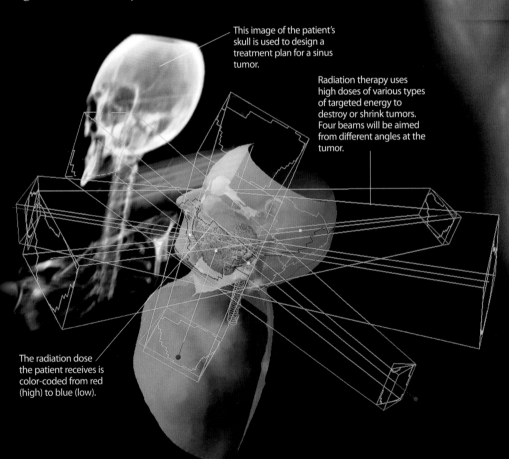

This image of the patient's skull is used to design a treatment plan for a sinus tumor.

Radiation therapy uses high doses of various types of targeted energy to destroy or shrink tumors. Four beams will be aimed from different angles at the tumor.

The radiation dose the patient receives is color-coded from red (high) to blue (low).

DESTROYING CANCER CELLS ▲

During the radiation therapy shown here, a special machine moves around the patient's body, aiming high-energy rays at the tumor. Although this treatment targets the cancer cells, some nearby healthy cells may also be damaged. In contrast, chemotherapy drugs are swallowed or injected, so the patient's whole body is exposed to them. That's why chemo usually

▼ ROBODOC

Scientists are developing many promising new cancer treatments. Some researchers are creating drugs that block the formation of the blood vessels that nourish cancer cells. Other researchers are developing microscopic devices, called *nanorobots*, that are injected into a patient's body to find, diagnose, and treat cancer cells.

Powered with chemical "engines," nanorobots will not only locate cancer cells but also show whether a cancer has spread.

Scientists intend to use nanorobots to inject chemotherapy drugs directly into cancer cells, without damaging healthy cells. They could also be used to deliver radiation therapy and even to perform surgery.

Cancer cell

CATAPULTS

What do a kangaroo, a fishing lure, and a pole-vaulter have in common? They are all launched into the air with the help of a simple machine: the lever. A lever that is used to throw things is called a *catapult*. If you have ever put a marshmallow in a plastic spoon, bent the spoon back, and then let go, you've operated a catapult. Levers, like seesaws, lift things. If a lot of force is applied quickly to one arm, the lever not only lifts but also throws whatever is on the other arm. Most catapults have one long arm and one short one. They were used as ancient weapons to hurl large stones or other objects at enemies. A stone would be placed on the end of the long arm. When many people pulled a rope attached to the short arm, the long arm swung up, launching the stone up and at the enemy.

The pole is made of strong materials so that it springs back with great force when bent.

Australian Sophie Lichoudaris pole vaults during a 2009 athletic festival in Sydney.

POLE VAULT ▶

In the sport of pole vault, athletes use a long pole to launch themselves over a raised bar. Holding one end of the pole, the athlete runs toward the bar and places the far end of the pole in the ground just below the bar. The pole becomes a long lever that swings the athlete up and over the bar.

CASTING LONG ▼

A fishing rod uses the power of the catapult to cast a lure out into the water, and then uses the rod as a lever to haul in a fish. The angler's right hand acts as the balance point, called the *fulcrum*. With a quick motion, he pushes on the short arm of the catapult with his left hand. The rod pivots around his right hand, lifting the lure into the air and flinging it out across the water. If a fish bites, the rod becomes a lever that lifts the catch out of the water.

A hopping kangaroo can travel more than 35 miles (56 km) per hour.

The long, heavy tail helps the animal balance.

KANGAROO HOPS ▲

Kangaroos' legs use a lever action to launch them 30 feet (9 m) through the air. They have an especially long and springy Achilles tendon, which is a rubbery band that attaches leg muscles to heel bones. The tendon stores and releases energy so effectively that kangaroos get more bounce and use less energy when they speed up their hopping.

The raised bar is set to release easily, preventing injury should the athlete bump into it.

Two vertical poles hold up the bar.

did you
know? ....
POLEVAULTER SERGEI BUBKA CLEARED A 20-FOOT (6 M) BAR—ABOUT THE HEIGHT OF A TWO-STORY HOUSE WITHOUT THE ROOF.

DK EDUCATION

Design Miranda Brown and Ali Scrivens, The Book Makers
Managing Art Editor Richard Czapnik
Design Director Stuart Jackman
Publisher Sophie Mitchell

PEARSON

The people who made up the *DK Big Ideas of Science Reference Library* team—representing digital product development, editorial, editorial services, manufacturing, and production—are listed below.

Johanna Burke, Jessica Chase, Arthur Ciccone, Amanda Ferguson, Kathryn Fobert, Christian Henry, Sharon Inglis, Russ Lappa, Dotti Marshall, Robyn Matzke, Tim McDonald, Maria Milczarek, Célio Pedrosa, Stephanie Rogers, Logan Schmidt, Christine Whitney

CREDITS